Best of
MALAYSIAN COOKING

Best of MALAYSIAN COOKING

Betty Saw

Marshall Cavendish Cuisine

The publisher wishes to thank Lim's Arts and Living, Sia Huat Pte Ltd and Madam Hamidah Omar for the loan and use of their tableware and kitchen utensils.

Photography: Joshua Tan
Food Preparation: Gourmet Haven

First published as Rasa Malaysia, 1982
Reprinted 1990, 1992, 1994, 1995, 1999, 2001, 2005
Published as The Complete Malaysian Cookbook, 2009, reprinted 2011
Published as Best of Malaysian Cooking, 2014
This new edition 2018

Published by Marshall Cavendish Cuisine
An imprint of Marshall Cavendish International

A member of the Times Publishing Group

Other Marshall Cavendish Offices:
Marshall Cavendish Corporation. 99 White Plains Road, Tarrytown NY 10591-9001, USA • Marshall Cavendish International (Thailand) Co Ltd. 253 Asoke, 12th Floor, Sukhumvit 21 Road, Klongtoey Nua, Wattana, Bangkok 10110, Thailand • Marshall Cavendish (Malaysia) Sdn Bhd, Times Subang, Lot 46, Subang Hi-Tech Industrial Park, Batu Tiga, 40000 Shah Alam, Selangor Darul Ehsan, Malaysia.

National Library Board, Singapore Cataloguing-in-Publication Data

Name(s): Saw, Betty. | Tan, Joshua, photographer.
Title: Best of Malaysian cooking / Betty Saw ; photography: Joshua Tan.
Other title(s): Rasa Malaysia
Description: Singapore : Marshall Cavendish Cuisine, 2018. | Originally published as Rasa Malaysia, 1982. Republished as The complete Malaysian cookbook, 2009. Republished as Best of Malaysian cooking, 2014.
Identifier(s): OCN 1026403156 | ISBN 978-981-48-2812-3 (paperback)
Subject(s): LCSH: Cooking--Malaysian. | LCGFT: Cookbooks.
Classification: DDC 641.59595--dc23

Printed in Malaysia

PREFACE

Have you ever lived in Malaysia? Stopped over? Perhaps you live here. A steady rhythm is apparent after a while. It is there in the serenity and languor of the country and suburbs, in the continuity of lifestyle of the rural people — a secure, timeless quality to be savoured in their industry, their daily rounds, and not less in their food and the way they serve it.

Malaysian cuisine is rich in its variety — the result of multicultural influences, both past and cosmopolitan present. The blend is exotic: Malay, Chinese, Peranakan, Indian, Eurasian. Yet, paradoxically, there is a unique taste attributable to the distinctive way of cooking in each particular state.

In this book, I shall introduce those intriguing tastes peculiar to the various states as we go through some of the Malaysian favourites enjoyed by everyone. There are also traditional specialties gathered firsthand from many dear *makciks* and *neneks*. Their epicurean capabilities, total recall and *agak-agak* culinary skills are rare. The ability of the older generation to lavish tender care in the preparation of their specialties and their enduring patience in so doing are qualities that deserve emulation.

For easy reference, I have attempted a systematic grouping of states, from south to north of Peninsular Malaysia, and then to East Malaysia. This is not done with any bias in mind and should not be taken as a reflection of the order of importance of the nation's states. Malaysian cities have varied Eastern and Western cuisines, as well as delightful arrays of provincial fare and Chinese food. For this reason, I have included a few recipes for Chinese favourites in Malaysia.

In the process of writing this book, I have derived immense pleasure and satisfaction discovering for myself the infinite possibilities in style and preparation that make cooking a constantly challenging endeavour. Discover this heritage of Malaysian cooking with me. I believe you will find the journey rewarding and enjoyable.

Betty Saw

CONTENTS

Negeri Sembilan

Selangor

Pahang

Perak

Kelantan

Terengganu

Penang

Kedah

Perlis

Sabah & Sarawak

HELPFUL HINTS

Banana Leaves

To soften banana leaves for wrapping *kuih*, either scald in boiling water or pass quickly over flame. If time permits, sun banana leaves for two hours for improved fragrance.

Bitter Gourd

To prepare bitter gourd, first scrape off the seeds and membrane inside, then soak cut pieces in salted water to reduce their bitter taste.

Black Prawn Paste

Like dried prawn (shrimp) paste (*belacan*), black prawn paste (*hae ko*) is made from prawns, but unlike solid dried prawn paste, it is a thick and gooey liquid. To use, it is usually taken straight out of the jar and diluted with a little warm water.

Blender (Processor) or Chopper

As far as possible, make full use of these time-saving gadgets. The electric chopper does a fine job, even with chilli seeds. If you feel the result is still not fine enough, use a grinding stone to refine.

A good liquidizer does an excellent job, except with chilli seeds. Also, frying the blended ingredients will take a little longer because of the extra water added. Always remember to slice ingredients, especially lemon grass and galangal, before blending, chopping or pounding.

Candlenuts

The Malay name for candlenuts is *buah keras*. The hard, oily nuts are available shelled or unshelled, and they are used to thicken some curries and make them more *lemak*, a Malay term for "richly creamy". If unavailable, use cashew nuts as a substitute.

Cloud Ear Fungus

Not to be confused with black (wood ear) fungus, cloud ear fungus is smaller and more delicate. Dark brown to black in colour, cloud ear fungus is sold dried and has to be soaked to soften before use.

Coconut Cream and Milk

Coconut cream is the first extraction of liquid from grated coconut after adding a little or no water. Coconut milk is the second extraction of liquid after adding considerably more water to the already once-squeezed grated coconut. *Pati santan* refers to pure coconut cream that has been extracted without adding any water. The best way to derive *pati santan* is by squeezing the grated coconut, a little at a time, using a piece of fine muslin cloth.

Grated coconut kept in the refrigerator or freezer will not yield as much as freshly grated coconut. Ideally, extract the required amount of milk, add a pinch of salt, then freeze. Frozen this way, it can be kept for as long as a week. However, if you do not have the time to extract coconut cream or milk before freezing, thaw frozen grated coconut and add hot water.

Cumin and Fennel Seeds

Cumin seeds are smaller and darker than fennel seeds. Both are essential ingredients in most curries, but cumin is usually used in smaller quantities than fennel.

Curry Powder

If a recipe calls for curry powder for the various meats, use your favourite brand. Ensure that it is fresh and fragrant, however, and remember to mix it with a little water before frying so as to prevent it from sticking to the pan. If it does stick before being well fried, sprinkle in a little water.

Fresh Chicken Stock

Stock obtained from boiling the bony parts of chicken like the claws, wing tips, neck, etc. in water over low heat.

Ground Ingredients

A good non-stick pan is ideal for frying these as the ingredients have to be fried in oil over low heat until fragrant and the oil separates to form a layer on the surface. Ground ingredients can always be prepared in advance and frozen in airtight containers to be used when required.

Kaffir Lime Leaf
The Chinese name for this unique fragrant leaf is horrendous. *Fat fong kum yip* literally means "leper leaf" and the name is probably due to the rough stubbly skin of the fruit. The leaf is sometimes called double lime leaf and is commonly used in curries and Malay *rendang*, a type of dish involving a thick gravy and pieces of meat.

Kerisik
Grated coconut, pan-fried without oil over low heat until brown and pounded or blended to a fine paste. This can be frozen for as long as two weeks.

Lemon Grass
A tall grass that grows quite easily in clumps. Discard the leaves and use about 10–12 cm from the thick root end. For grinding, the outer layer is usually removed before use. When a recipe calls for lightly crushed lemon grass, smash lightly with a pestle or the flat surface of a cleaver.

Local Beef
If it is not one of the tender cuts, score meat lightly with the blunt edge of a cleaver. Meat should always be cut across the grain.

Palm Sugar
Also known as *gula Melaka*, palm sugar is dark brown and sold in the form of cylindrical or round cakes wrapped in dried leaves. It is made from the sap of coconut palm flowers and has a lovely fragrance. To melt palm sugar, chop cake into smaller pieces first. Once melted into syrup, strain to remove grit.

Roasted Peanuts
Made from shelled raw peanuts and pan-fried dry over low heat, stirring constantly until golden brown. Rub off the thin brown skins then winnow in a flat tray or basket. After cooling, they store well in an airtight container in the refrigerator.

Screwpine Leaves
Dark green in colour, screwpine or *pandan* leaves are used for their special fragrance. *Kuih* and sweets made with coconut milk simply will not be the same without these aromatic leaves.

Seasoning a New Earthen Pot
Soak the earthen pot in water, preferably overnight. Put in a whole coconut, grated, and fry over low heat until coconut is dry and brown. Discard coconut and rinse the pot.

Shallot Crisps or Crisp-fried Shallots
Slice shallots thinly crosswise. Heat enough oil for deep-frying and stir shallots over low heat until pale brown. Remove with a perforated ladle and drain on absorbent paper. When cool, store in an airtight container. Shallot crisps keep well for several weeks in the refrigerator. (Garlic crisps are prepared the same way.)

Tahi Minyak
When *pati santan* or pure coconut cream is cooked over low heat, stirring constantly for quite some time, it thickens and eventually oil separates, leaving a residue. The Malays call this *tahi minyak*. Drained from oil, this residue is crisp and rich brown, and is often used in a dessert or *sambal* (chilli paste).

Torch Ginger Bud
Sometimes called wild ginger flower, the torch ginger bud has a lovely fragrance and comes from a tall, wild ginger plant that resembles that of galangal. The bud is typically sold with several inches of stem attached. Do not discard the stem, but use by smashing lightly with the flat surface of a cleaver to get the full fragrance.

Johor

Occupying the entire southern portion of the Malay peninsula, as well as rich with pineapple plantations and oil palm and rubber estates, is Johor State. Johor Bahru, its modern capital city, is situated at the southernmost tip and is connected to the island-state of Singapore by two busy causeways.

Johor has a strong Malay culture and Malay cuisine is interestingly varied with a taste of Javanese. Laksa Johor or Laksa Bersantan, Mee Rebus and Sayur Lodeh, an enticing mixed vegetable curry, are some of the tempting favourites to match healthy appetites.

The Chinese population in Johor is mainly Teochew and some of their popular offerings are Teochew Duck, Five-spice Meat Rolls and Steamed Fish Teochew Style. Teochew cooking is generously spiced with five-spice powder and is renowned for its variety of braised meats in dark soy sauce, normally eaten with bland porridge or flat rice noodles.

Acar Rampai

Preparation: 15 minutes Cooking: 12 minutes

Ingredients

Cucumbers	2, seed portions discarded, cut into 4 x 0.6-cm strips
Carrot	1, large, peeled and cut into 4 x 0.6-cm strips
Preserved radish (*chye poh*)	2 Tbsp, washed and chopped
Shallots	14, peeled; 10 halved and 4 sliced
Garlic	6 cloves, peeled and halved
Red chillies	4, seeded and cut into strips
Green chillies	4, seeded and cut into strips
Ginger	150 g, peeled and shredded
Salt	1 tsp
Sugar	1 tsp
Ground turmeric (*kunyit serbuk*)	1 tsp
Mustard seeds	1 dsp, washed and drained
Cooking oil	5 Tbsp
Sultanas	1 Tbsp

Ingredients to be ground

Dried chillies	20
Turmeric (*kunyit*)	2.5-cm knob, peeled

Ingredients to be combined

Vinegar	125 ml
Water	65 ml
Sugar	1 dsp
Salt	1/4 tsp

Method

- Into a mixing bowl, put cucumbers, carrot, preserved radish, shallot halves, garlic, chillies and ginger. Mix well with salt, sugar and ground turmeric. Leave for 1 hour. Drain well of collected vegetable juices before use.
- Heat a dry wok and fry mustard seeds for 1 minute. Remove and set aside.
- Add oil to heated wok and when hot, lightly brown sliced shallots. Then, add ground ingredients and fry until oil separates.
- Add combined ingredients and bring to the boil. Simmer gently for 3 minutes, then add in prepared vegetables, mustard seeds and sultanas.

Note: If short of time, lightly squeeze vegetables using a piece of cloth to remove vegetable juices instead of waiting an hour for them to emerge.

Ikan Masam Manis

Preparation: 10 minutes Cooking: 25 minutes

Ingredients

Black pomfret (*ikan bawal hitam*)	600 g
Cooking oil	as needed
Shallots	3, peeled and sliced
Garlic	2 cloves, peeled and sliced
Ginger	2.5-cm knob, peeled and cut into strips
Water	250 ml
Carrot	1/2, small, peeled if desired and cut into 4-cm strips
Red chillies	2, seeded and cut into strips
Coriander leaves (cilantro) for garnishing	

Batter (combined)

Plain (all-purpose) flour	2 Tbsp
Ground white pepper	1/2 tsp
Salt	1/2 tsp
Water	2 Tbsp

Seasoning (combined)

Light soy sauce	2 dsp
Vinegar	2 dsp
Sugar	1 tsp
Salt	1/2 tsp
Cornflour (cornstarch)	1 tsp

Method

- Wash fish and make 2 slits across on each side.
- Coat fish with combined batter ingredients, then deep-fry until light brown and crisp. Drain fish and place on a serving dish.
- Heat 2 Tbsp oil in a wok. Fry shallots, garlic and ginger until fragrant, then add water.
- When liquid reaches the boil, add carrot and chillies. Simmer for 5 minutes before adding combined seasoning ingredients.
- Pour hot gravy on top of fish and garnish, if desired, with coriander.

Gulai Ikan Pedas

Preparation: 15 minutes Cooking: 15 minutes

Ingredients

Wolf herring (*ikan parang*)	600 g, cut into 7.5-cm slices
Salt	1 1/2 tsp
Cooking oil	4 Tbsp
Shallots	5, peeled and sliced
Garlic	3 cloves, peeled and sliced
Tamarind pulp (*asam Jawa*)	2 Tbsp, mixed with 750 ml water and strained
Salted cabbage (*kiam chye*)	180 g, sliced and soaked
Sugar	1 tsp

Ingredients to be ground

Dried chillies	30, soaked
Shallots	5, peeled
Garlic	3 cloves, peeled
Ginger	2.5-cm knob, peeled
Dried prawn (shrimp) paste (*belacan*)	1.25-cm square piece
Ground turmeric (*kunyit serbuk*)	1 tsp

Method

- Clean fish, rub with 1 tsp salt and set aside.
- Heat oil in a wok and lightly brown shallots and garlic.
- Add ground ingredients and fry until fragrant, then add tamarind juice and bring to the boil.
- Add salted cabbage and simmer for 2 minutes.
- Add 1/2 tsp salt, sugar and fish. Cook until fish is done.

Panggang Ikan Terubuk

Preparation: 10 minutes Grilling: 20 minutes

Ingredients

Hilsa or shad (*ikan terubuk*)	600 g
Salt	1/2 tsp
Cooking oil	

Chilli Tamarind Sauce (combined)

Bird's eye chillies (*cili padi*)	15–20, ground
Shallots	5, peeled and sliced
Sugar	1 tsp
Tamarind pulp (*asam Jawa*)	2 tsp, mixed with 3 Tbsp water and strained
Salt	1/4 tsp or to taste

Method

- Wash and clean fish; remove entrails but not the scales. Rub body cavity with 1/2 tsp salt and brush with oil.
- Grill fish over glowing coals or under a preheated grill. For the latter, line tray with foil. Grill fish for 10 minutes on each side, brushing with more oil.
- Serve hot with chilli tamarind sauce as dip.

Note: Hilsa or shad (*ikan terubuk*) is full of fine bones and has a special flavour of its own. Keeping the scales when grilling or pan-frying this fish helps to impart and preserve that special flavour.

Teochew Steamed Fish

Preparation: 15 minutes Steaming: 15 minutes
Cooking: 3 minutes

Ingredients

Fish	600–900 g, preferably threadfin (*ikan kurau/ senangin*), white or Chinese pomfret (*ikan bawal putih* or *tambak*)
Salt	1 1/2 tsp
Ground white pepper	1 tsp
Salted cabbage (*kiam chye*)	120 g, soaked in water and sliced
Dried Chinese mushrooms	4, soaked to soften, stems discarded and cut into strips
Chicken or pork	90 g, cut into strips
Ginger	4-cm knob, peeled and cut into strips
Red chillies	2, cut into strips
Pickled sour plums	2
Sesame oil	1 tsp
Water	125 ml
Cooking oil	1 Tbsp
Shallots	3–4, peeled and sliced

Garnishing

Spring onions (scallions)	2, cut into 5-cm lengths
Coriander leaves (cilantro)	2 sprigs, cut into 5-cm lengths

Method

- Clean fish thoroughly, then rub with salt and pepper.
- Place fish onto a heatproof dish. Distribute salted cabbage, mushrooms, chicken or pork, ginger and chillies over and around fish.
- Lightly squeeze sour plums and place beside fish. Add sesame oil and water.
- Prepare a steamer for use. When water is rapidly boiling, place dish into steamer and steam for 15 minutes.
- Meanwhile, heat oil a wok. Fry shallot slices until lightly browned, then set aside.
- When fish is cooked, pour oil and shallots over fish. Serve garnished.

Otak-Otak Tenggiri

Preparation: 25 minutes Cooking: 20 minutes Makes 16 packets

Ingredients

Spanish mackerel (*ikan tenggiri*)	600 g, central portion
Salt	3 tsp
Eggs	5
Coconut cream	250 ml, squeezed from 1 grated coconut with a little water added
Banana leaves	
Bamboo toothpicks or cocktail sticks	

Ingredients to be ground

Dried chillies	15, soaked
Bird's eye chillies (*cili padi*)	10
Shallots	5, peeled
Garlic	2 cloves, peeled
Lemon grass (*serai*)	2 stalks
Galangal (*lengkuas*)	3 slices, peeled
Dried prawn (shrimp) paste (*belacan*)	1.25-cm square piece
Ground turmeric (*kunyit serbuk*)	1 tsp

Ingredients to be finely sliced

Kaffir lime leaves (*daun limau purut*)	3
Turmeric leaves (*daun kunyit*)	2
Pointed pepper leaves (*daun kaduk*)	20

Method

- Wash and fillet fish, then cut fillets into 5 x 4-cm pieces. Season fish pieces with 1 tsp salt and leave for 15 minutes.
- Beat eggs lightly with a fork and stir in ground ingredients and finely sliced leaves. Mix in coconut cream and 2 tsp salt. Set aside.
- Run banana leaves over flame or a heated electric stove until softened, then cut into 18 x 15-cm pieces. Make sure cut leaves have no holes or slits or gravy will seep through. Wash and dry prepared leaves.
- On the centre of each banana leaf rectangle, put a piece of fish. Then, lift 2 long sides and bring them together over fish.
- Fold in one end by pushing lower edge 90° upwards so a triangular flap forms on either side. Fold flaps toward the centre before adding in 2 Tbsp egg mixture. Then, fold in the other end and fasten parcel with a toothpick or cocktail stick.
- Trim off excess leaf at parcel's top to neaten. Repeat until ingredients are used up.
- Steam parcels for 20 minutes.

Sotong Masak Hitam

Preparation: 20 minutes Cooking: 15 minutes

Ingredients

Squid	600 g, small–medium
Salt	2 tsp
Cooking oil	1 Tbsp
Onions	2, peeled and sliced into rings
Red chillies	2, seeded and sliced

Ingredients to be coarsely ground

Shallots	5, peeled
Garlic	3 cloves, peeled
Turmeric (*kunyit*)	2.5-cm knob, peeled
Ginger	2.5-cm knob, peeled

Method

- Wash and clean each squid, removing entrails. Keep whole and leave eyes intact.
- Rub cleaned squid with 1 tsp salt and leave for 15 minutes.
- Heat oil in a wok and fry ground ingredients until fragrant.
- Add squid and simmer over low heat for 10 minutes.
- Add all remaining ingredients and season with 1 tsp salt. Stir-fry for 2–3 minutes.

Note: This dish may look unappetisingly black but it is *sedap*, which is Malay for "tasty", when eaten with rice.

Kari Kambing

Preparation: 15 minutes Cooking: 1 hour

Ingredients

Mutton or beef	600 g
Cooking oil	4 Tbsp
Coconut cream	500 ml, squeezed from 1 grated coconut with a little water added
Coconut milk	750 ml, squeezed from the same grated coconut with sufficient water added
Potatoes	4, peeled and quartered
Tomatoes	3, halved
Salt	1 1/2 tsp

Spices

Cinnamon (*kayu manis*)	2.5-cm stick
Cardamoms (*buah pelaga*)	3
Cloves (*bunga cengkih*)	6
Star anise (*bunga lawang*)	2 sections

Ingredients to be ground

Shallots	8, peeled
Garlic	3 cloves, peeled
Ginger	5-cm knob, peeled
Galangal (*lengkuas*)	2.5-cm knob, peeled
Meat curry powder	5 Tbsp

Method

- Cut mutton or beef into thin slices. Set aside.
- Heat oil in a pot and fry whole spices for a few minutes. Add ground ingredients and fry until fragrant and oil separates.
- Add meat slices and stir. When slices are well coated with curry paste, add coconut milk and bring to the boil. Then, simmer gently for 40 minutes or until meat is almost tender.
- Add potatoes, then tomatoes. Pour in coconut cream and simmer until meat is tender and gravy thick.
- Season with salt.

Teochew Duck

Preparation: 10 minutes Cooking: 50 minutes

Ingredients

Young duck	1, about 1.5 kg
Salt	2 dsp to rub inside duck and 1 dsp to rub outside duck
Five-spice powder	1 Tbsp
Galangal (*lengkuas*)	150 g, peeled and sliced
Cooking oil	1/2 Tbsp
Sugar	1 rounded (heaped) Tbsp
Water	750 ml
Garlic	3 cloves, peeled
Cinnamon (*kayu manis*)	7.5-cm stick
Sichuan peppercorns	8
Dark soy sauce	4 Tbsp

Method

- Rub inside and outside of duck with salt, then five-spice powder. Stuff duck with galangal slices. Set aside.
- Heat oil in a wok. Add sugar and cook until dark golden, then add water and bring to the boil.
- Add all remaining ingredients and duck. Add enough water to cover three-quarters of duck.
- Cover and simmer for about 45 minutes or until sauce is dark and thick and duck tender.
- Cut duck into serving-size pieces and pour sauce over.

Sayur Lodeh

Preparation: 20 minutes Cooking: 20 minutes

Ingredients

Cooking oil	4 Tbsp
Dried prawns (shrimps) (*hae be*)	120 g, ground
Coconut cream	250 ml, squeezed from 1 grated coconut with a little water added
Coconut milk	1 litre, squeezed from same grated coconut with sufficient water added
Firm bean curd (*tau kwa*)	2 pieces, cut into small cubes
Salt	2 tsp or to taste

Ingredients to be ground

Red chillies	15
Shallots	12, peeled
Garlic	2 cloves, peeled
Dried prawn (shrimp) paste (*belacan*)	2.5-cm piece
Candlenuts (*buah keras*)	5
Ground turmeric (*kunyit serbuk*)	1 tsp

Vegetables

Carrot	1, cut into 4 x 1.25-cm strips
Yam bean (*bangkuang*)	360 g, cut into 4 x 1.25-cm strips
Cabbage leaves	4–5, cut into 4-cm pieces
Aubergines (eggplants/brinjals)	2, diagonally cut into 1.25-cm thick slices
Long (snake) beans	8, cut into 4-cm lengths

Method

- Heat oil in a wok and fry ground ingredients until fragrant.
- Add dried prawns and stir for a few minutes before adding a little coconut cream to prevent sticking.
- When ingredients are fragrant, add coconut milk and bring to the boil.
- Add vegetables and bean curd. When liquid returns to the boil, reduce heat and simmer until vegetables are tender.
- Add remaining coconut cream and salt to taste.

Nasi Minyak

Preparation: 15 minutes Cooking: 30 minutes

Ingredients

Thai rice	3.5 kg
Ghee (clarified butter)	4 Tbsp
Shallots	7, peeled and sliced
Garlic	4 cloves, peeled and sliced
Ginger	5-cm knob, peeled and shredded
Water	1.875 litres
Evaporated milk	1 small can (170 g)
Salt	1 Tbsp
Chinese celery	3 stalks, cut into 2.5-cm lengths

Spices

Cloves (*bunga cengkih*)	8
Cardamoms (*buah pelaga*)	4
Cinnamon (*kayu manis*)	2.5-cm stick

Method

- Wash and drain rice, then put into a rice cooker.
- Heat ghee in a wok. Lightly brown shallots, garlic and ginger, then add spices and fry for 2 minutes until fragrant.
- Add water, evaporated milk and salt and bring to the boil.
- Add Chinese celery and pour mixture into rice cooker. Cook until rice is done.
- Serve hot with meat and fish curries accompanied with a plain mixed vegetable salad or *acar timun* (page 30).

Note: To make *nasi biryani*, follow the same recipe but use biryani rice instead of Thai rice, and add a few sprigs of mint leaves with Chinese celery. When rice is boiling and half-cooked, stir in a few drops of yellow colouring or a few saffron strands mixed with a little milk.

Satay Daging

Preparation: 1 hour Grilling: 45 minutes Makes 85–90 sticks

Ingredients

Beef	1 kg
Satay sticks or bamboo skewers	85–90, soaked in water for 2 hours
Lemon grass (*serai*)	1 stalk, thicker end crushed for basting

Marinade

Sugar	6 rounded (heaped) tsp
Light soy sauce	1$^1/_2$ Tbsp
Salt	1 Tbsp
Cooking oil	2 Tbsp

Ingredients to be finely ground

Lemon grass (*serai*)	4 stalks, sliced
Turmeric (*kunyit*)	4-cm knob, peeled
Fennel seeds (*jintan manis biji*)	1 tsp
Cumin seeds (*jintan putih biji*)	$^3/_4$ tsp

Ingredients to be combined

Pure coconut cream (*pati santan*)	squeezed from 1 grated coconut
Cooking oil	3–4 Tbsp

Method

- Ask your butcher for a tender cut for *satay*. Slice beef into 4 x 2-cm pieces, each about 0.6-cm thick.
- Marinate meat with combined marinade and finely ground ingredients for at least 2 hours.
- Onto each pre-soaked *satay* stick or skewer, thread several pieces of meat to cover 7.5 cm from the top. Repeat until ingredients are used up.
- Dip crushed, splayed end of lemon grass into combined ingredients and brush mixture onto skewered meat.
- Grill meat over glowing coal on both sides, basting with combined ingredients several times until meat is well done.
- Serve hot with satay peanut sauce (page 26), *ketupat* or *nasi himpit* (page 31), which are compressed rice cakes, and cucumber and onion wedges.

Satay Ayam

Preparation: 40 minutes Grilling: 25–30 minutes
Makes 30–35 sticks

Ingredients

Chicken meat	600 g, from 1 medium chicken or 4 drumsticks
Salt	2 tsp
Sugar	4 rounded (heaped) tsp
Light soy sauce	1 Tbsp
Cooking oil	1 Tbsp
Satay sticks or bamboo skewers	30–35, soaked in water for 2 hours before use
Lemon grass (*serai*)	1 stalk, thicker end crushed for basting

Ingredients to be ground

Lemon grass (*serai*)	3 stalks, sliced
Turmeric (*kunyit*)	2.5-cm knob, peeled
Garlic	2 cloves, peeled

Ingredients to be combined

Pure coconut cream (*pati santan*)	squeezed from 1/2 grated coconut
Cooking oil	2 Tbsp

Method

- Slice chicken into 2.5 x 1.25-cm pieces.
- Into a mixing bowl, put chicken, ground ingredients, salt, sugar, light soy sauce and oil. Mix well and leave to marinate for 2 hours.
- Onto each pre-soaked *satay* stick or skewer, thread on enough meat to cover 7.5 cm and grill as for satay daging (page 24).
- Serve hot with satay peanut sauce (recipe on right), *ketupat* or *nasi himpit* (page 31), which are compressed rice cakes, and cucumber and onion wedges.

Note: Soaking the satay sticks or skewers in water for a couple of hours will prevent the ends from burning during grilling.

Satay Peanut Sauce

Preparation: 30 minutes Cooking: 20 minutes

Ingredients

Cooking oil	4 Tbsp
Roasted peanuts	180 g, coarsely ground
Coconut cream	375 ml, squeezed from 1 grated coconut with a little water added
Tamarind pulp (*asam Jawa*)	2 tsp, mixed with 125 ml water and strained
Sugar	2 tsp
Salt	1 1/2 tsp

Ingredients to be ground

Dried chillies	15, seeded
Garlic	2 cloves, peeled
Shallots	12, peeled
Lemon grass (*serai*)	1 stalk, sliced
Coriander seeds (*ketumbar biji*)	1 Tbsp
Fennel seeds (*jintan manis biji*)	1 tsp
Cumin seeds (*jintan putih biji*)	3/4 tsp
Candlenuts (*buah keras*)	5
Dried prawn (shrimp) paste (*belacan*)	1.25-cm square piece

Method

- Heat oil in a wok. Fry ground ingredients until fragrant and oil separates.
- Add ground peanuts, then coconut cream and bring to a slow boil.
- Add tamarind juice, sugar and salt. Simmer for 5 minutes more.

Note: Kajang satay might be better known for its sauce, but Johor satay is second to none in its preparation.

Kurma Ayam

Preparation: 15 minutes   Cooking: 40 minutes

Ingredients

Chicken	1, about 1.5 kg, cut into 4 large pieces
Salt	2 1/2 tsp
Cooking oil	4 Tbsp
Kurma curry powder	125 g, mixed with water into a paste
Water	750 ml
Evaporated milk	4 Tbsp
Potatoes	4, peeled and halved
Onions	2, peeled and quartered
Coriander leaves (cilantro)	1 small sprig, cut into 5-cm lengths
Tomatoes	4, halved

Ingredients to be ground

Poppy seeds	1 rounded (heaped) dsp
Shallots	10, peeled
Garlic	4 cloves, peeled
Ginger	5-cm knob, peeled

Garnishing

Red chillies	2, split lengthways
Peas	1 Tbsp, boiled

Method

- Season chicken with 1 tsp salt. Set aside.
- Heat oil in a pot. Fry combined curry paste and ground ingredients until fragrant and oil separates.
- Add water and bring to a slow boil, then add chicken.
- Cover and simmer over moderate heat for 15 minutes.
- Uncover pot to add evaporated milk, potatoes and onions.
- Simmer until ingredients are cooked and gravy is thick.
- Mix in all remaining ingredients and season with 1 1/2 tsp salt. Serve garnished.

Rojak Suun

Preparation: 30 minutes   Cooking: 15 minutes

Ingredients

Transparent (glass) noodles (*tang hoon*)	300 g
Bean sprouts	300 g
Potatoes	600 g
Cooking oil for deep-frying	
Firm bean curd (*tau kwa*)	5
Cucumbers	3, sliced
Chinese lettuce	2 small bunches
Salt	2 tsp
Vinegar	1 Tbsp
Sugar	2 tsp

Ingredients to be ground

Dried chillies	15, soaked
Dried prawns (shrimps) (*hae be*)	150 g, washed, dried and toasted
Sesame seeds	1 Tbsp, toasted
Garlic	3 cloves, peeled

Method

- Scald transparent noodles, then bean sprouts in boiling water. Drain.
- Boil potatoes until cooked, then peel and cut into small cubes.
- Heat sufficient oil for deep-frying and cook bean curd until light brown. Halve each piece, then slice across.
- Into a mixing bowl, put prepared noodles, bean sprouts, potatoes and bean curd, as well as cucumbers. Mix well, then transfer to a serving dish garnished with lettuce leaves.
- Just before serving, combine ground ingredients with salt, vinegar and sugar and mix well before pouring over noodles and vegetables.

Sambal Ikan with Belimbing

Preparation: 10 minutes Cooking: 15 minutes

Ingredients

Spanish mackerel (*ikan tenggiri*)	450 g, preferably head portion
Salt	as needed
Blimbing (*belimbing*)	8
Cooking oil	2 Tbsp
Red chillies	2, seeded and diagonally sliced
Lemon grass (*serai*)	1 stalk, crushed
Coconut milk	500 ml, squeezed from ½ grated coconut with sufficient water added
Sugar	1 tsp

Ingredients to be ground

Red chillies	6, seeded
Dried chillies	10, soaked
Shallots	10, peeled
Candlenuts (*buah keras*)	3
Dried prawn (shrimp) paste (*belacan*)	2.5 x 1.25-cm piece

Method

- Season fish with 1 tsp salt and leave for 10 minutes.
- Rub blimbing with 1/4 tsp salt and set aside.
- Heat oil in a wok. Fry ground ingredients, chilli slices and lemon grass until fragrant and oil separates.
- Add coconut milk, blimbing, sugar and 1/2 tsp salt, then bring to a slow boil.
- Add fish and simmer for 5 minutes or until cooked.

Note: Relatives of the sweet yellow star fruit, blimbing, are green in colour, sour-tasting and quite small, about the size of a thumb. If unavailable, substitute with 1 Tbsp lemon juice.

Rojak Tauhu

Preparation: 15 minutes Cooking: 20 minutes

Ingredients

Cooking oil	as needed
Raw shelled peanuts	300 g
Firm bean curd (*tau kwa*)	5–6 pieces
Bean sprouts	240 g, tailed and scalded
Cucumbers	2, peeled and cut into small wedges
Bird's eye chillies (*cili padi*)	35
Garlic flakes	2 tsp
Palm sugar (*gula Melaka*)	60 g, chopped
Kalamansi limes (*limau kesturi*)	8
Water	315 ml
Sugar	1 Tbsp
Salt	1 tsp

Method

- Heat 3 Tbsp oil in a wok. Fry peanuts until light golden, then drain from oil. Rub skins off cooled peanuts before coarsely pounding. Set aside.
- Heat sufficient oil for deep-frying and cook bean curd until lightly browned on both sides, then drain. Cut cooled bean curd into small cubes.
- Combine scalded bean sprouts, cucumber wedges and fried bean curd cubes on a serving dish. Pour *rojak* sauce over vegetables just before serving.
- Prepare *rojak* sauce. Combine bird's eye chillies and garlic flakes in a blender (food processor) or a mortar using a pestle. Transfer to a mixing bowl. Add ground peanuts and palm sugar, then squeeze in lime juice through a strainer and mix well. Stir in all remaining ingredients.

Acar Timun

Preparation: 15 minutes Cooking: 8 minutes

Ingredients

Cucumbers	3, peeled and coarsely shredded
Carrot	1, coarsely shredded
Shallots	15, peeled and sliced
Ginger	5-cm knob, peeled and shredded
Red chillies	3, diagonally sliced
Salt	1 Tbsp
Garlic flakes	1 Tbsp, lightly crushed
Cooking oil	3 Tbsp
Dried chillies	12, soaked and ground
Ground turmeric (*kunyit serbuk*)	1 tsp

Ingredients to be combined

Tomato sauce (ketchup)	3 Tbsp
Water	1 Tbsp
Sugar	2 Tbsp
Vinegar	2 dsp
Salt	1 tsp

Method

- Into a mixing bowl, put cucumbers, carrot, shallots, ginger and chillies. Mix well with salt.
- Wrap mixed vegetables with a piece of fine muslin cloth. Place a heavy weight on top and leave overnight.
- On cooking day, vegetables should be very crisp because water has since drained away. Transfer vegetables from cloth to a bowl and stir in garlic flakes. Set aside.
- Heat oil in a wok. Fry ground chillies and ground turmeric for 3 minutes, then add combined ingredients.
- When liquid reaches the boil, add crisp mixed vegetables. Stir-fry to mix well for 1 minute.
- Serve as an accompaniment to *nasi minyak* (page 23).

Note: If you have forgotten to prepare the vegetables overnight, remove vegetable juice by lightly squeezing them using a piece of muslin cloth instead. Garlic flakes are available in most Chinese sundry shops.

Soto Ayam

Preparation: 45 minutes Cooking: (Rice) 30 minutes; (25 Burgers) 20 minutes; (Soup) 45 minutes

Ingredients

Nasi himpit (rice cakes)*	1 recipe
Beef burgers**	1 recipe
Chicken soup***	1 recipe
Bean sprouts	450 g, tailed and scalded in boiling water for 1 minute

Garnishing

Shallots	300 g, peeled, sliced and crisp-fried in oil (reserve 2 Tbsp of this oil)
Chinese celery	4 sprigs, chopped

Method

- Prepare rice cakes, beef burgers and chicken soup.
- To serve, put some rice, bean sprouts, burgers and chicken meat into individual serving bowls. Ladle hot soup over and garnish.
- Serve hot, and if desired, with a dipping sauce of 40 ground bird's eye chillies (*cili padi*) and 3 Tbsp light soy sauce combined.

*Nasi Himpit (Rice Cakes)

Rice	600 g
Water	1.065 litres
Salt	a pinch

Method

- Wash and drain rice. Put into a rice cooker with water and salt. Cook until rice is done.
- Stir and mash cooked rice with a wooden spoon while still hot, then transfer to a 25 x 15-cm rectangular container with a flat lid a little bit smaller than the rim.
- Press smaller lid firmly onto rice and place a heavy object on top to compress rice. Refrigerate overnight.
- When done, cut into 2.5-cm cubes and set aside.

**Beef Burgers

Potatoes	600 g, peeled, boiled and mashed
Minced beef	300 g
Ground white pepper	1 Tbsp
Salt	1 1/2 tsp
Shallots	10, peeled, sliced and lightly browned in oil
Eggs	2, beaten
Plain (all-purpose) flour	
Cooking oil for shallow-frying	

Method

- Into a mixing bowl, put potatoes and beef. Mix well with pepper, salt and fried shallots, then stir in beaten eggs.
- With wet hands, shape mixture into patties 5 cm in diameter and lightly roll in flour.
- Shallow-fry floured patties for about 5 minutes or until cooked. Quarter cooled burgers.

***Chicken Soup

Water	3.75 litres
Ginger	5-cm knob, peeled and lightly crushed
Garlic	4 cloves, peeled
Chicken	1, about 1.5 kg, halved
Salt	2 tsp
Shallot oil	2 Tbsp, reserved from frying shallot slices for garnishing

Spices (combined)

Cinnamon (*kayu manis*)	7.5-cm stick
Star anise (*bunga lawang*)	5 sections
Cardamoms (*buah pelaga*)	2
Black peppercorns	10
White peppercorns	1 rounded (heaped) tsp
Coriander seeds (*ketumbar biji*)	1 tsp
Fennel seeds (*jintan manis biji*)	1/2 tsp
Cumin seeds (*jintan putih biji*)	1/2 tsp

Method

- Wrap spices with a piece of cloth and secure with string. Lightly crush spice bag with a pestle, then prick with a skewer.
- Into a large pot, put water, ginger, garlic and spice bag. Bring to a slow boil.
- Add chicken, cover and simmer for 30 minutes or until chicken is tender.
- Add salt. Remove scum from liquid surface and add shallot oil.
- Drain chicken and tear slightly cooled meat into small pieces. Arrange on a serving dish.

Sambal Goreng Tempeh

Preparation: 20 minutes Cooking: 25 minutes

Ingredients

Fermented soy bean cake (tempeh)	4 pieces
Cooking oil for deep-frying	
Firm bean curd (*tau kwa*)	4 pieces
Transparent (glass) noodles (*tang hoon*)	45 g
Prawns (shrimps)	450 g, peeled and deveined
Salt	as needed
Cooking oil	3 Tbsp
Onion	1, large, peeled and sliced
Red chillies	2, seeded and diagonally sliced
Green chillies	2, seeded and diagonally sliced
Tamarind pulp (*asam Jawa*)	1 rounded (heaped) tsp, mixed with 65 ml water and strained
Coconut milk	750 ml, squeezed from 1 grated coconut with sufficient water added
Long (snake) beans	150 g, cut into 4-cm lengths

Ingredients to be ground

Dried chillies	15, soaked
Shallots	15, peeled
Garlic	5 cloves, peeled
Turmeric (*kunyit*)	2.5-cm knob, peeled
Dried prawn (shrimp) paste (*belacan*)	2.5 x 1.25-cm piece

Method

- Cut preserved soy bean cake into 2.5-cm pieces and deep-fry in hot oil until lightly browned. Drain and set aside.
- Quarter each firm bean curd and deep-fry. Remove and drain.
- Wash and drain transparent noodles, then deep-fry. Remove and drain.
- Season peeled prawns with $^1/_2$ tsp salt and leave aside.
- Heat 4 Tbsp oil in a wok and brown onion slices. Add ground ingredients and chilli slices. Fry until fragrant and oil separates.
- Add prawns and stir-fry for 2 minutes, then add tamarind juice and coconut milk. Bring to a slow boil.
- Add long beans, as well as fried soy bean cakes, firm bean curd and transparent noodles. Simmer over low heat until long beans are cooked. Season with $1^1/_2$ tsp salt.
- Serve with rice.

Note: Fermented soy bean cake (tempeh) comes in rectangular packets and are easily available at Malay stalls in markets. They are usually wrapped in banana leaves or *daun ketapang*. When fresh from the market, they can be kept in the refrigerator for 2–3 days. When they are not fresh, they turn a mouldy black.

Nasi Dhal Berhias

Preparation: 15 minutes Cooking: 25 minutes

Ingredients

Thai rice	600 g
Lentils	300 g, soaked, preferably overnight
Cooking oil	1 Tbsp
Ghee (clarified butter)	1 Tbsp
Onions	2, peeled and chopped
Ginger	2.5-cm knob, peeled and chopped
Water	1 litre
Evaporated milk	1 small can (170 g)
Salt	2 dsp

Spices

Cloves (*bunga cengkih*)	5
Cinnamon (*kayu manis*)	2.5-cm long stick
Star anise (*bunga lawang*)	3 sections
Cardamoms (*buah pelaga*)	5

Garnishing (optional)

Crisp-fried shallots

Hard-boiled egg slices

Method

- Wash rice and drain well. Set aside.
- Wash soaked lentils thoroughly, discarding those that float on the surface. Drain in a colander.
- Heat oil and ghee in a wok. Brown onions and ginger, then add spices and stir-fry for 1–2 minutes or until fragrant. Transfer fried ingredients to a rice cooker.
- Add water and evaporated milk to rice cooker and stir to mix. Allow liquid to reach the boil before adding rice and lentils. Mix well, adding salt. Cook rice for about 20 minutes.
- Garnish, if desired, and serve hot with *kari kambing* (page 22), *kurma ayam* (page 27) or *acar rampai* (page 14).

Syrup Bandung

Preparation: 5 minutes Cooking: 5 minutes Makes 1 litre

Ingredients

Water	500 ml
Sugar	120 g
Screwpine (*pandan*) leaves	3, knotted
Evaporated milk	1 small can (170 g)
Salt	1 pinch
Red food colouring	2–3 drops
Ice cream soda	1 large bottle (1.25 litres)

Method

- In a saucepan, bring water, sugar and screwpine leaves to the boil. Cook until sugar dissolves, then remove and leave to cool. Discard screwpine leaves.
- Combine cooled syrup with all remaining ingredients and mix well. Serve thoroughly chilled.

Note: Syrup *bandung* is popularly served as a refreshing drink at Malay wedding feasts.

Kuih Bakar Jagung

Preparation: 15 minutes Baking: 50 minutes Makes 21

Ingredients

Sweet corn	1 can (450 g)
Coconut milk	665 ml, squeezed from 1 1/2 grated coconuts with sufficient water added
Plain (all-purpose) flour	240 g
Sugar	195 g
Eggs	4, lightly beaten with a fork
Margarine	1 Tbsp, melted
Vanilla essence (extract)	1 tsp
Margarine for greasing	

Method

- Put sweet corn and a little coconut milk into a blender (food processor). Blend until fine and set aside.
- Sift flour into a mixing bowl, add sugar and stir in remaining coconut milk, a little at a time, until smooth. If batter is lumpy, put it through a strainer.
- Stir in eggs, blended sweet corn, melted margarine and vanilla essence.
- Grease individual *kuih bakar* patty tins with margarine. Fill patty tins with batter and bake in an oven preheated to 175°C/350°F for 50 minutes or until tops are lightly browned.
- Allow to cool before turning out. Loosen *kuih* by running a round-bladed knife along edge of patty tin. *Kuih bakar* will sink slightly at the centre with cooling.

Note: If *kuih bakar* patty tins are unavailable, use cupcake patty tins which are slightly shallower.

Five-spice Meat Rolls

Preparation: 30 minutes Cooking: 5 minutes
Steaming: 12 minutes

Ingredients

Minced chicken	600 g, including 2 pieces chicken fat, or minced streaky pork
Small prawns (shrimps)	300 g, peeled and minced
Crabmeat	240 g
Spring onions (scallions)	2–3, chopped
Egg	1/2, beaten
Plain (all-purpose) flour	1 Tbsp
Bean curd skin (*fu pei*)	1 large sheet, cut into 30 x 12.5-cm pieces
Plain (all-purpose) flour paste	
Cooking oil for deep-frying	

Ingredients to be coarsely minced

Carrot	10-cm piece
Water chestnuts	6
Dried Chinese mushrooms	5, soaked to soften and stems discarded

Seasoning

Five-spice powder	1/2 tsp
Salt	1/2 tsp
Ground white pepper	1/2 tsp
Light soy sauce	1/2 Tbsp
Sesame oil	1/2 Tbsp

Garnishing

Cucumber slices
Tomato slices

Method

- Place meat, prawns, crabmeat, spring onions and coarsely minced ingredients in a mixing bowl. Mix with seasoning ingredients, egg and flour. Leave for 1 hour.
- Onto the centre of each piece of soy bean skin, put enough marinated meat mixture and roll up; resulting rolls should be 4 cm in diameter. Dab a little flour paste on edges to seal.
- Steam rolls over rapidly boiling water for 12 minutes. Using a sharp knife, cut steamed rolls into 2.5-cm wide pieces.
- Heat oil for deep-frying in a wok until hot. Cook rolls until light golden brown. Serve garnished.

Laksa Johor Bersantan

Preparation: 20 minutes Cooking: 30 minutes

Ingredients

Skinned coconuts	2, grated
Dried sour fruit (*asam gelugur*)	3–4 pieces
Salt	2 tsp
Wolf herring (*ikan parang*)	1.25 kg, steamed and flaked
Fresh thick round rice (*laksa*) noodles	1.25 kg, scalded

Ingredients to be ground

Dried chillies	40, soaked and seeded
Shallots	15, peeled
Turmeric (*kunyit*)	2.5-cm knob, peeled
Lemon grass (*serai*)	3 stalks
Galangal (*lengkuas*)	12 slices, peeled
Black peppercorns	1 tsp
Dried prawn (shrimp) paste (*belacan*)	5 x 2.5-cm piece

Garnishing

Bean sprouts	300 g
Cucumber	1, peeled and shredded
Mint leaves	

Method

- Reserve 1 cup grated coconut for *kerisik* (page 11). With sufficient water added, squeeze remaining coconut for 3 litres coconut milk.
- Into a clay pot, put ground ingredients, coconut milk, dried sour fruit, salt, flaked fish and *kerisik*. Bring to the boil, then simmer over low heat for 15 minutes, stirring occasionally.
- To serve, put some scalded noodles into individual serving bowls and top with a little of each garnishing ingredient. Ladle gravy over and serve hot.

Mee Siam Kering

Preparation: 30 minutes Cooking: 20 minutes

Ingredients

Dried rice vermicelli (*bee hoon*)	600 g
Cooking oil	175 ml
Shallots	20, peeled and sliced
Firm bean curd (*tau kwa*)	2 pieces, cut into small cubes
Onion	1, peeled and ground
Small prawns (shrimps)	300 g, peeled
Beef	240 g, thinly sliced
Salt	2 tsp
Eggs	2, lightly beaten
Chinese flowering cabbage (*chye sim*)	3 stalks, stems and leaves separated, cut into 5-cm lengths and stems lightly smashed
Bean sprouts	300 g
Chinese (garlic) chives	10–12 stalks, cut into 2.5-cm lengths
Chinese celery	3 sprigs, chopped

Ingredients to be ground

Dried chillies	15, soaked
Dried prawns (shrimps)	3 Tbsp

Garnishing

Red chillies	3, sliced
Green chillies	3, sliced
Kalamansi limes (*limau kesturi*)	10, halved

Method

- Soak vermicelli in water for 10 minutes until soft. Drain in a colander.
- Heat oil in a wok. Fry shallot slices until golden brown. Remove with a perforated ladle and set aside.
- In the same oil, fry bean curd until lightly browned, then remove and set aside.
- Still in the same oil, fry ground onion until fragrant, then add ground ingredients and stir-fry until fragrant.
- Add prawns, then beef and salt. Pour in beaten eggs and quickly stir-fry.
- Add Chinese flowering cabbage, stems first then leaves. Stir-fry before adding fried bean curd and rice vermicelli. Mix well.
- Add bean sprouts and Chinese chives and fry briskly for 2 minutes. Lastly, add half the chopped Chinese celery.
- Place on a large dish and garnish with remaining Chinese celery, crisp-fried shallots and garnishing ingredients.

Kuih Koleh-koleh Kacang

Preparation: 15 minutes Cooking: 1 hour 10 minutes

Ingredients

Green (mung) beans	300 g, soaked for at least 2 hours or preferably overnight
Water	1 litre
Coconut cream	750 ml, squeezed from $1\frac{1}{2}$ grated coconuts with a little water added
Palm sugar (*gula Melaka*)	450 g, cut into small pieces
Water	125 ml
Screwpine (*pandan*) leaves	2
Banana leaf (optional)	1
Topping (*tahi minyak*)*	1 recipe

Method

- Wash green beans and put into a pressure cooker with 1 litre water. Pressure cook for 20 minutes.
- Transfer cooked green beans to a blender (food processor), add coconut cream and blend until fine. For easier and finer blending, do this a third at a time. If blender is not turning well, add a little extra coconut cream.
- Into a small saucepan, put palm sugar and 125 ml water. Cook, stirring frequently, until sugar dissolves. Strain into blended beans. Mix well.
- Pour bean mixture into a wok, add screwpine leaves and, using a wooden spatula, stir continuously over low heat for 15 minutes or until a thick paste results. Do not allow mixture to stick to bottom of wok.
- To test that paste is thick enough, make a figure '8' with the spatula, and if it holds well, paste is of the right consistency. Discard screwpine leaves.
- Spoon paste into an 27 x 18-cm shallow tin and smooth surface while still hot with a piece of banana leaf or a butter knife. Sprinkle on topping and leave to cool thoroughly before cutting.

*Topping (***Tahi Minyak***)

Ingredients

Pure coconut cream (*pati santan*)	250 ml, squeezed from 1 grated coconut

Method

- Put coconut cream into a wok and stir over low heat with a wooden spatula for 30–35 minutes. Oil will separate from coconut residue.
- Continue stirring until coconut residue turns a rich brown. Remove from heat and strain oil from coconut residue crisps.

Note: Green bean flour, if available, can be used instead. Simply sift flour and stir in coconut cream without adding water. If *kuih koleh-koleh* turns out to be your favourite as it is mine, then it is worth the effort to wash as much as 2–3 kilograms of beans, during your spare time of course, pan-fry or oven toast until dry, then send to the mill for grinding. It keeps well for months, especially in the refrigerator.

To wash green beans and thoroughly remove small stones and grit, wash and scoop beans with fingers into a separate container instead of draining water away from pan. This way the heavier sand and grit will remain at the bottom of the pan. Repeat this process several times.

Coconut residue crisps when drained from oil and cooled can be stored in an airtight container for as long as a week without refrigeration. A tablespoon or two of this added to *sambal* prawns, prawns cooked in chilli paste, with slightly thicker gravy imparts a delightful flavour.

Mee Rebus

Preparation: 40 minutes Cooking: 50 minutes

Ingredients

Cooking oil	5 Tbsp
Beef	300 g, thinly sliced
Rice flour	3 Tbsp, mixed with a little water to make thickener
Sugar	1 Tbsp
Salt	2 tsp
Fresh yellow (*Hokkien*) noodles	600 g, scalded in boiling water
Bean sprouts	300 g, tailed and scalded in boiling water

Ingredients to be ground

Dried chillies	20, seeded
Shallots	30, peeled
Garlic	4 cloves, peeled
Turmeric (*kunyit*)	5-cm knob, peeled
Galangal (*lengkuas*)	2.5-cm knob, peeled
Black peppercorns	40
Preserved soy beans (*tau cheo*)	2 Tbsp

Ingredients to be blended (processed)

Coconut milk	3 litres, squeezed from 1 grated coconut with sufficient water added
Sweet potatoes	900 g, peeled and steamed
Small prawns (shrimps)	600 g, peeled

Garnishing

Hard-boiled eggs	5, shelled and quartered
Spring onions (scallions)	4, chopped
Green chillies	5, sliced
Kalamansi limes (*limau kesturi*)	10, halved
Prawn (shrimp) crisps*	1 recipe, lightly crushed

Method

- Heat oil in a wok. Fry ground ingredients until fragrant and oil separates.
- Add beef and fry for 2 minutes, then pour in blended ingredients. Bring to a slow boil, reduce heat and simmer for 5–10 minutes.
- Add thickener, then sugar and salt. When gravy returns to the boil, turn off heat. Reheat just before serving.
- To serve, put some noodles and bean sprouts into individual serving bowls. Ladle hot gravy over and top with a little of each garnishing ingredient.

*Prawn Crisps

Plain (all-purpose) flour	6 Tbsp, sifted
Water	9 Tbsp
Salt	1/2 tsp
Ground prawns (shrimps)	1 Tbsp
Cooking oil for deep-frying	

Method

- Combine flour and water for a smooth batter. Except oil, stir in all other ingredients.
- Heat oil in a wok until hot. Spoon a tablespoon of batter into hot oil, carefully spreading out batter. Fry over medium heat until golden brown.
- Drain on absorbent paper and keep in an airtight container until serving time.

Kuih Nagasari

Preparation: 30 minutes Cooking: 30 minutes Makes 16

Ingredients

Rice flour	240 g
Water	500 ml
Coconut milk	875 ml, squeezed from 1 grated coconut with sufficient water added
Screwpine (*pandan*) leaves	2, knotted
Salt	1/2 tsp
Banana leaves	16, cut into 18 x 15-cm pieces, scalded
Small ripe bananas (*raja* variety)	8, peeled and halved lengthways

Method

- Sift rice flour into a bowl, add water and blend until smooth.
- Into a saucepan, put coconut milk, screwpine leaves and salt. Bring to a slow boil.
- Add rice batter to coconut milk and stir with a wooden spoon for about 5 minutes or until mixture becomes a smooth paste. Remove from heat.
- Onto the centre of each banana leaf, place a dessertspoonful of cooked mixture. Fold over one side of banana leaf to flatten and shape mixture into a small rectangle.
- Unfold leaf, top with a banana half and cover with another spoonful of cooked mixture.
- Fold banana leaf in thirds lengthways, overlapping to cover mixture. Then, fold 2 short ends under so parcel's weight rests on them.
- Steam parcels for 20 minutes. Serve hot or cold.

Note: Some brands of rice flour contain a percentage of tapioca flour, which hardens the *kuih*. To avoid this, add more coconut milk to the batter.

Melaka

Steeped in history, Melaka is Malaysia's oldest and historically most important city, though not much of its history before the fourteenth century is known. Founded by a Malay noble in that century, it flourished and attracted traders from near and far for spices, silks, ivory and gold. Admiral Cheng Ho forged the first link with Melaka and eventually the Chinese settled there. At the turn of the century, Melaka fell to the Portuguese who were to remain for some 130 years, making the port one of the mightiest fortresses in the east. Melaka then fell to the Dutch and they held the city for more than a century and a half.

The distinct legacy of this historic and picturesque past is inherent in the wide variety of food one is fortunate to savour in Melaka, very often an exciting and rich potpurri of Malay, Nyonya and Portuguese foods.

Malay food is deliciously hot and sour — like Ikan Masak Kuah Lada, Daging Masak Asam Tumis and Ikan Masak Lemak. Nyonya food, a blend of Chinese and Malay cuisines, is cooked Malay style with lots of coconut milk, spices, chillies and fragrant roots and grasses. However, Chinese ingredients such as pork, dried Chinese mushrooms and soy sauce are used, giving the typically Nyonya Ayam or Babi Pong Tay, Ayam Tempra and Ayam Sioh. Portuguese-influenced dishes are sour and spicy, with generous use of tamarind as well as vinegar. Dishes like Feng, Pada, Chicken Debal Curry and Chicken Vindaloo are popular within the community and, though not as well known as other cuisines, are tantalisingly delicious.

Ikan Bawal Masak Kuah Lada

Preparation: 15 minutes Cooking: 20 minutes

Ingredients

Black pomfret (*ikan bawal hitam*)	1, medium, cut into 4–5 pieces
Salt	2 tsp
Cooking oil	3 Tbsp
Lemon grass (*serai*)	2 stalks, lightly crushed
Salted cabbage (*kiam chye*)	180 g, sliced
Tamarind pulp (*asam Jawa*)	2 rounded (heaped) dsp, mixed with 1 litre water and strained

Ingredients to be ground

White peppercorns	30 g
Candlenuts (*buah keras*)	5
Shallots	6, peeled
Garlic	4 cloves, peeled
Dried prawn (shrimp) paste (*belacan*)	2.5 x 1.25-cm piece
Turmeric (*kunyit*)	1.25-cm knob, peeled

Method

- Rub fish with 1 tsp salt and leave for 15 minutes.
- In an earthen pot, heat oil and fry lemon grass for 2 minutes.
- Add ground ingredients and fry until fragrant.
- Add salted cabbage and stir-fry for 1–2 minutes.
- Pour in tamarind juice and bring to a slow boil.
- Add fish and 1 tsp salt. When fish is cooked, remove from heat.

Ikan Masak Kuah Lada

Preparation: 15 minutes   Cooking: 20 minutes

Ingredients

Wolf herring (*ikan parang*)	450 g, cut into 9-cm slices
Salt	2 tsp
Cooking oil	3 Tbsp
Grated skinned coconut	4 Tbsp, for *kerisik* (page 11), ground
Tamarind pulp	1 dsp, mixed with 375 ml water and strained

Ingredients to be ground

Red chillies	10, seeded
Shallots	8, peeled
Garlic	3 cloves, peeled
Coriander seeds (*ketumbar biji*)	2 Tbsp
Fennel seeds (*jintan manis biji*)	1 tsp
Black peppercorns	1 tsp
Ground turmeric (*kunyit serbuk*)	1 tsp

Method

- Rub fish with 1 tsp salt and leave for 15 minutes.
- Heat oil in a wok and fry ground ingredients until fragrant.
- Add *kerisik* and fry over low heat for 2 minutes, then add tamarind juice.
- When liquid reaches the boil, add fish and cook for 8–10 minutes or until fish is done.
- Stir in 1 tsp salt and remove from heat.

Ikan Masak Lemak

Preparation: 10 minutes   Grilling: 25–30 minutes
Cooking: 12 minutes

Ingredients

Horse mackerels (*ikan cupak*)	2
Salt	1 1/2 tsp
Coconut milk	500 ml, squeezed from 1 grated coconut with sufficient water added
Dried sour fruit (*asam gelugur*)	2 small pieces
Salted cabbage (*kiam chye*)	180 g, sliced

Ingredients to be ground

Dried chillies	12, soaked
Shallots	8, peeled
Ground turmeric (*kunyit serbuk*)	1 tsp

Method

- Wash fish but do not remove hard skins. Rub them with 1 tsp salt and grill each side for 15 minutes or until just cooked.
- Gently remove hard skin.
- Into an earthen pot, put ground ingredients, coconut milk and dried sour fruit. Bring to a slow boil.
- Add salted cabbage and simmer over low heat for 10 minutes.
- Add fish and 1/2 tsp salt. Cook for 2 minutes more and remove from heat.

Ikan Garam Asam

Preparation: 15 minutes Cooking: 15 minutes

Ingredients

Black pomfret (*ikan bawal hitam*) or Spanish mackerel (*ikan tenggiri*)	600 g
Salt	2 tsp
Cooking oil	4 Tbsp
Blimbing (*belimbing*)	6, halved lengthwise
Tamarind pulp (*asam Jawa*)	3 Tbsp, mixed with 500 ml water and strained
Sugar	1 dsp

Ingredients to be ground

Red chillies	12
Dried chillies	10, soaked
Lemon grass (*serai*)	1 stalk
Galangal (*lengkuas*)	2.5-cm knob, peeled
Turmeric (*kunyit*)	2.5-cm knob, peeled
Dried prawn (shrimp) paste (*belacan*)	1.25-cm square piece
Candlenuts (*buah keras*)	8

Method

- Season fish with 1 tsp salt and leave for 15 minutes.
- In an earthen pot, heat oil and fry ground ingredients until fragrant.
- Add blimbing and stir-fry for 1 minute, then add tamarind juice, a little at a time, whilst frying.
- Bring to the boil, then reduce heat and simmer for 5 minutes.
- Add sugar, 1 tsp salt and fish and cook until fish is done.

Fried Tamarind Prawns

Preparation: 5 minutes Cooking: 5 minutes

Ingredients

Large prawns (shrimps)	600 g
Tamarind pulp (*asam Jawa*)	2 rounded (heaped) Tbsp, mixed with 4 Tbsp water and strained
Salt	1 tsp
Ground white pepper	1/2 tsp
Sugar	1/2 tsp
Cooking oil	250 ml
Cucumber	1, sliced

Method

- Trim off eye portions and legs of prawns, but leave unpeeled.
- In a mixing bowl, combine thick tamarind juice, salt, pepper and sugar. Mix in prawns and leave for 15 minutes.
- Heat oil in a wok until hot. Fry prawns over moderate heat for 3–5 minutes or until prawns are cooked.
- Arrange prawns on a serving dish garnished with cucumber slices.

Pada (Salted Fish Pickle)

Preparation: 15 minutes Cooking: 40 minutes

Ingredients

Salted fish	600 g, preferably threadfin (*ikan kurau/senangin*)
Cooking oil	375 ml
Vinegar	500 ml
Tamarind pulp (*asam Jawa*)	3 Tbsp, mixed with 65 ml water and strained
Sugar	240 g, boiled in 65 ml water until dissolved

Ingredients to be ground

Shallots	15, peeled
Garlic	4 whole pods, peeled
Ginger	7.5-cm knob, peeled
Vindaloo curry powder (page 66)	5 Tbsp, mixed with 5 Tbsp water into a paste

Method

- Wash and drain salted fish, then cut into 2-cm square pieces. Leave pieces to dry in the sun for 2 hours.
- Heat oil in a wok. Deep-fry salted fish over low heat for 7–10 minutes or until golden brown and crisp. Drain from oil.
- Strain oil from wok into an earthen pot, then place over heat.
- When oil is hot, fry ground ingredients over low heat until fragrant.
- Add vinegar, tamarind juice and sugar syrup. Bring to a slow boil and simmer for 12–15 minutes or until gravy is thick and a thick layer of oil separates.
- Cool gravy thoroughly before adding in fried salted fish. Store in airtight jars.

Note: Salted fish pickle keeps well, for as long as a year, in the refrigerator. It goes well with rice and is delicious as a sandwich spread. Instead of salted fish, fresh fish, preferably Spanish mackerel (*ikan tenggiri*), can be used. Deep-fry fish slices until cooked then pour prepared gravy over fish.

Squid in Tamarind

Preparation: 15 minutes Cooking: 20 minutes

Ingredients

Squid	450 g, small–medium
Tamarind pulp (*asam Jawa*)	3 Tbsp, mixed with 625 ml water and strained
Dried prawn (shrimp) paste (*belacan*)	1.25-cm square piece
Sugar	1 dsp
Salt	1 tsp
Dried sour fruit (*asam gelugur*)	3 pieces
Shallots	12, peeled and sliced
Lemon grass (*serai*)	2 stalks, crushed
Red chillies	4, stems retained and split lengthways
Green chillies	4, stems retained and split lengthways

Method

- Wash and clean squids, removing entrails and ink sacs.
- Except chillies and squids, put all other ingredients into a pot. Bring to the boil.
- Add chillies and simmer gently for 10 minutes.
- Add squids and cook for 3–4 minutes or until just cooked.

Rendang Daging Lembu

Preparation: 20 minutes Cooking: 1 hour 30 minutes

Ingredients

Beef	600 g
Coconut milk	1.25 litres, squeezed from 1 1/2 grated coconuts with sufficient water added
Skinned coconut	1/2, grated, for *kerisik* (page 11)
Turmeric leaves (*daun kunyit*)	2
Salt	1 1/2 tsp

Ingredients to be ground

Dried chillies	15, soaked
Coriander seeds (*ketumbar biji*)	3 Tbsp
Fennel seeds (*jintan manis biji*)	1 tsp
Black peppercorns	1 tsp
Lemon grass (*serai*)	4 stalks
Shallots	12, peeled
Galangal (*lengkuas*)	4-cm knob, peeled
Ginger	4-cm knob, peeled

Method

- Cut beef into 0.6-cm thick slices and drain in a colander.
- Into an earthen pot, put beef, ground ingredients and coconut milk. Bring to a slow boil and simmer gently for 1 hour 15 minutes, stirring frequently, until gravy is thick.
- Add *kerisik*, turmeric leaves and salt. Continue stirring until gravy is almost dry and meat tender.

Daging Masak Asam Tumis

Preparation: 20 minutes   Cooking: 45 minutes

Ingredients

Beef	600 g
Cooking oil	4 Tbsp
Lemon grass (*serai*)	2 stalks, lightly crushed
Galangal (*lengkuas*)	4-cm knob, lightly crushed
Tamarind pulp (*asam Jawa*)	2 rounded (heaped) dsp, mixed with 500 ml water and strained
Salt	$1\frac{1}{2}$ tsp or to taste

Ingredients to be ground

Dried chillies	30, soaked
Shallots	15, peeled
Garlic	3 cloves, peeled
Turmeric (*kunyit*)	2.5-cm knob, peeled

Method

- Cut meat into 0.6-cm thick slices and drain in a colander.
- In an earthen pot, heat oil and fry ground ingredients until fragrant and oil separates.
- Add beef slices and stir-fry for a few minutes.
- Add lemon grass, galangal and tamarind juice. Bring to the boil and simmer gently for 30 minutes or until meat is tender and gravy thick.
- Stir in salt to taste.

Beef Semur (Stew)

Preparation: 15 minutes   Cooking: 1 hour 15 minutes

Ingredients

Beef	600 g, cut into 5 x 2.5 x 2.5-cm chunks
Ground white pepper	1 dsp
Light soy sauce	2 Tbsp
Dark soy sauce	1 tsp
Vinegar	2 Tbsp
Cooking oil	2 Tbsp
Onions	2, large, peeled and sliced
Hot water	1.5 litres
Potatoes	4, peeled and kept whole
Salt	1 tsp

Spices

Cloves (*bunga cengkih*)	4
Nutmeg (*buah pala*)	$\frac{1}{4}$ piece
Cinnamon (*kayu manis*)	2.5-cm stick

Method

- Season beef with pepper, both soy sauces and vinegar. Leave for 30 minutes.
- Heat oil in a pot or wok and fry onions until transparent.
- Add spices and fry until fragrant, then add beef and stir for a few minutes.
- Pour in hot water and bring to the boil before reducing heat. Cover and simmer for 1 hour, stirring occasionally.
- Halfway through cooking, add potatoes and salt.

Sambal Udang Kering

Preparation: 15 minutes Cooking: 30 minutes

Ingredients

Dried prawns (shrimps)	300 g
Cooking oil	3 Tbsp
Tamarind pulp (*asam Jawa*)	2 Tbsp, mixed with 65 ml water and strained
Sugar	1 tsp
Shallots	8, peeled, sliced and crisp-fried

Ingredients to be ground

Dried chillies	35, soaked
Shallots	240 g, peeled
Lemon grass (*serai*)	6 stalks, sliced
Turmeric (*kunyit*)	1.25-cm knob, peeled

Method

- Soak dried prawns in water for 30 minutes. Rinse, drain and squeeze dry.
- Either blend (process) prepared dried prawns or pound them using a mortar and pestle until fine.
- Heat oil in a wok until hot. Fry ground ingredients over low heat for a few minutes or until fragrant.
- Add ground prawns, then thick tamarind juice and sugar. Stir-fry continuously until dry, then remove from heat.
- When cool, mix in crisp-fried shallots. Transfer to airtight jars to store.

Note: Sambal udang kering keeps well in the refrigerator. It is delicious with toasted bread or as a sandwich spread.

Semur (Oxtail Stew)

Preparation: 15 minutes Cooking: 50 minutes

Ingredients

Oxtail	1 kg, cut into 4-cm pieces
Water	2.25 litres
Cooking oil	2 Tbsp
Onions	2, peeled and sliced
Light soy sauce	1 Tbsp
Dark soy sauce	1 tsp
Potatoes	4, medium, peeled and halved
Salt	1 1/2 tsp
Vinegar	1 tsp

Ingredients to be ground

Cinnamon (*kayu manis*)	2.5-cm stick
Cloves (*bunga cengkih*)	5
Nutmeg (*buah pala*)	1/4 piece

Method

- Into a pressure cooker, put oxtail and water. Cook for 30 minutes.
- Heat oil in a cooking pot or wok and fry onions until transparent. Add ground spices and fry until fragrant.
- Add cooked oxtail and liquid from pressure cooker. Bring to the boil.
- Add both soy sauces and potatoes. Simmer over low heat until potatoes are cooked.
- Add salt and vinegar.

Ayam Tempra

Preparation: 15 minutes Cooking: 25 minutes

Ingredients

Chicken	1 kg, cut into bite-size pieces
Salt	1 tsp
Cooking oil	3 Tbsp

Ingredients to be sliced

Shallots	15, peeled
Onions	3, peeled
Red chillies	4

Sauce (combined)

Water	250 ml
Dark soy sauce	2 Tbsp
Sugar	1 Tbsp
Salt	1 tsp

Method

- Season chicken with salt and set aside.
- Heat oil in a wok and fry sliced ingredients until fragrant and transparent.
- Add chicken and stir-fry over high heat for 5–7 minutes or until chicken is lightly browned.
- Add combined sauce ingredients and bring to the boil, then cover and simmer for 15–20 minutes or until chicken is tender and sauce thick.

Devil

Preparation: 20 minutes Cooking: 25 minutes

Ingredients

Chicken	1.5 kg, cut into bite-size pieces
Salt	as needed
Cooking oil	4 Tbsp
Onions	2, peeled and sliced
Mustard seeds	1 Tbsp
Rice vinegar	6 Tbsp
Water	315 ml
Potatoes	3, peeled and quartered

Ingredients to be ground

Dried chillies	10, soaked
Red chillies	6
Shallots	12, peeled
Garlic	5 cloves, peeled
Ginger	2.5-cm knob, peeled
Turmeric (*kunyit*)	2.5-cm knob, peeled
Candlenuts (*buah keras*)	8

Method

- Season chicken with 1 tsp salt and set aside.
- Heat oil in a wok and lightly brown onions, then add ground ingredients and fry for 5 minutes.
- Add mustard seeds and rice vinegar. Bring to a slow boil.
- Add chicken and fry for a few minutes, then add water.
- When liquid reaches the boil, reduce heat, add potatoes and simmer until chicken is tender and potatoes cooked.
- Add salt to taste.

Note: This version of Devil is delicious using leftover roast chicken or roast pork. Add 1 Tbsp coriander to ground ingredients and 125 ml water or gravy from meat, if available.

Chicken Vindaloo

Preparation: 15 minutes Cooking: 30 minutes

Ingredients

Chicken, pork or beef	1 kg
Cooking oil	4 Tbsp
Vindaloo curry powder (page 66)	3 Tbsp, mixed with a little water into a paste
Vinegar	125 ml
Water	250 ml
Salt	1½ tsp

Ingredients to be ground

Shallots	15, peeled
Garlic	10 cloves, peeled
Ginger	2.5-cm knob, peeled

Method

- Cut chicken into small pieces. If using pork or beef, cut into 0.6-cm thick slices.
- Heat oil in a pan and fry ground ingredients for 1 minute, then add curry paste and fry until fragrant and oil separates.
- Add vinegar, a little at a time, while frying combined ground ingredients and curry paste.
- Add meat and fry over high heat for a few minutes, then add water and salt.
- Simmer over low heat for 15 minutes or until meat is tender and gravy thick.

Note: Vindaloo is a Portuguese Indian dish from Kerala. If prepared *vindaloo* curry powder is unavailable, grind 20 pre-soaked dried chillies, 1½ Tbsp cumin and 2 tsp mustard seeds into a paste with shallots, garlic and ginger.

Feng (Curried Variety Meats)

Preparation: 1 hour Cooking: 45 minutes

Ingredients

Cow's or pig's intestine	300 g
Salt	as needed
Vinegar	as needed
Cow's or pig's lung	300 g, halved lengthways
Beef or pork	300 g
Cow's or pig's heart	300 g
Cow's or pig's liver	300 g
Cooking oil	175 ml
Ginger	5-cm knob, peeled and cut into strips

Ingredients to be ground

Coriander seeds (*ketumbar biji*)	2 Tbsp
Fennel seeds (*jintan manis biji*)	1 dsp
Cumin seeds (*jintan putih biji*)	1 dsp
White peppercorns	1 Tbsp
Dried turmeric (*kunyit kering*)	2.5-cm knob, peeled, or 1 tsp ground turmeric (*kunyit serbuk*)
Candlenuts (*buah keras*)	6
Shallots	10, peeled
Garlic	5 cloves, peeled

Method

- Turn intestine inside out using a chopstick, then rub with 2 tsp salt and some vinegar. Wash thoroughly, drain and set aside.
- Rub lung with 2 tsp salt and some vinegar, then wash thoroughly and drain.
- Into a pressure cooker, put prepared intestine and lung. Add some water and cook for 30 minutes or until tender.
- Drain cooked lung and intestine and leave to cool. Discard remaining liquid. Cut cooled lung and intestine into 0.6-cm cubes.
- Bring a saucepan of water to the boil. Add beef or pork and heart. Cook for 15 minutes, then drain and set aside.
- Into the same water, lower liver and cook for 5 minutes or until just done. Drain and leave to cool. Reserve 500 ml of liquid to use as stock later.
- Cut cooled beef or pork, heart and liver into 0.6-cm cubes. Set aside.
- Heat oil in a wok and lightly brown ginger. Drain strips from oil and set aside.
- Add ground ingredients to oil and fry over low heat until fragrant.
- Except liver, add all other diced ingredients and stir well.
- Add stock and bring to a slow boil, then reduce heat and simmer until meat is tender and very little liquid remains.
- Mix in diced liver, fried ginger strips, 3 tsp salt and 2 Tbsp vinegar.

Note: Feng is a traditional Portuguese Eurasian dish served for Christmas.

Ayam Goreng Rempah

Preparation: 15 minutes Cooking: 30 minutes

Ingredients

Chicken	1, 1.5 kg, cut into bite-size pieces
Ground turmeric (*kunyit*)	1 tsp
Salt	2 tsp
Cooking oil for deep-frying	
Turmeric leaf (*daun kunyit*)	1

Ingredients to be ground

Red chillies	10
Shallots	10, peeled
Garlic	5 cloves, peeled
Ginger	4-cm knob, peeled
Lemon grass (*serai*)	3 stalks
Coriander seeds (*ketumbar biji*)	3 Tbsp
Fennel seeds (*jintan manis biji*)	1 tsp
Black peppercorns	1 tsp

Method

- Season chicken with ground turmeric and 1 tsp salt. Leave for 30 minutes.
- Heat oil in a wok and deep-fry chicken for 15 minutes or until golden brown. Drain and set aside.
- Remove oil from wok, leaving behind about 2 Tbsp. Fry ground ingredients until fragrant and oil separates.
- Add turmeric leaf and fried chicken. Stir-fry over low heat until chicken is well coated with ground ingredients.
- Add remaining ingredients and season with 1 tsp salt before removing from heat.

Kacang Panjang Masak Lemak Udang

Preparation: 15 minutes Cooking: 20 minutes

Ingredients

Long (snake) beans	360 g
Small prawns (shrimps)	300 g, peeled
Salt	1/2 tsp
Cooking oil	3 Tbsp
Dried prawns (shrimps) (*hae be*)	60 g, soaked and coarsely ground
Coconut cream	250 ml, squeezed from 1 grated coconut with a little water added
Coconut milk	500 ml, squeezed from same grated coconut with sufficient water added

Ingredients to be ground

Red chillies	5
Shallots	6, peeled
Candlenuts (*buah keras*)	3
Dried prawn (shrimp) paste (*belacan*)	1.25-cm cube piece

Method

- Cut long beans into 5-cm lengths. Set aside.
- Season peeled prawns with salt and leave for 15 minutes.
- Heat oil in a wok. Fry ground ingredients for a few minutes, then add dried prawns and fry until fragrant.
- Add long beans and stir-fry for 1 minute, then pour in coconut milk. Bring to the boil and simmer for 5 minutes or until beans are just tender but not too soft.
- Add prawns and cook for 1 minute, then add coconut cream. When liquid returns to the boil, remove from heat.

Portuguese Acar

Preparation: 40 minutes Cooking: 20 minutes

Ingredients

Green chillies	450 g, stems retained
Slaked lime paste	1 Tbsp
Cucumber	1, quartered lengthwise, soft portions discarded, cut into 4-cm pieces
Salt	4 tsp
Cauliflower	240 g, cut into small pieces
Sugar	1 cup, mixed with 125 ml water
Mustard seeds	2 Tbsp, washed and dried in the sun
Cooking oil	100 ml
Vinegar	1.5 litres
Garlic	10 cloves, peeled, sliced and crisp-fried

Ingredients to be ground

Turmeric (*kunyit*)	7.5-cm knob, peeled
Dried prawns (shrimps) (*hae be*)	120 g, washed and drained

Method

- Wash green chillies in a basin of water mixed with slaked lime paste. Drain and wash thoroughly with water, then dry chillies with a clean cloth.
- Make a 5-cm slit from the stem end to the centre of each chilli and remove seeds, if desired. Set aside.
- Rub cucumber pieces with 2 tsp salt, then lightly squeeze to remove juice. Dry pieces in the sun for 2 hours.
- Sprinkle cauliflower pieces with 2 tsp salt and set aside.
- Into a small saucepan, put combined sugar and water. Bring to a slow boil and cook until sugar dissolves. Remove syrup from heat and set aside.
- Lightly crush mustard seeds and remove outer skins. Set aside.
- Heat oil in a pan and fry ground ingredients until fragrant.
- Add vinegar and bring to a slow boil, then add syrup and stir until liquid returns to the boil.
- Remove from heat and pour into a deep bowl. Allow vinegar mixture to cool completely.
- To cooled liquid, add prepared mustard seeds, green chillies, cucumber and cauliflower pieces, as well as crisp-fried garlic slices. Stir well and leave for 3 days before serving.

Ayam/Babi Pong Tay (Stewed Chicken or Pork)

Preparation: 15 minutes Cooking: 40 minutes

Ingredients

Chicken	1 kg, or 600 g streaky pork
Salt	1 tsp
Cooking oil	3 Tbsp
Preserved soy beans (*tau cheo*)	2 Tbsp
Dried Chinese mushrooms	4–5, soaked to soften and stems discarded
Water	500 ml
Dark soy sauce	1 tsp
Potatoes	3, peeled and quartered

Ingredients to be ground

Shallots	180 g, peeled
Garlic	3 whole pods, peeled

Method

- Cut chicken into small pieces. If using pork, cut into 5 x 2.5-cm pieces. Season meat with 1/2 tsp salt and set aside.
- Heat oil in a wok and fry ground ingredients for 2 minutes.
- Add preserved soy beans and fry over low heat until fragrant.
- Add mushrooms, then meat and stir-fry for a few minutes.
- Add water and dark soy sauce and bring to the boil. Reduce heat, cover and simmer for 15 minutes.
- Add potatoes and 1/2 tsp salt. Simmer gently for 12–15 minutes more or until meat is tender and sauce quite thick.

Chicken Debal Curry

Preparation: 20 minutes Cooking: 25 minutes

Ingredients

Chicken	1.5 kg, cut into bite-size pieces
Salt	2 tsp
Cooking oil	4 Tbsp
Mustard seeds	1 Tbsp, lightly crushed
Water	375 ml

Ingredients to be sliced

Shallots	6, peeled
Garlic	3 cloves, peeled
Red chillies	3

Ingredients to be ground

Dried chillies	30, soaked
Red chillies	5
Ginger	5-cm knob, peeled
Shallots	15, peeled
Garlic	3 cloves, peeled
Candlenuts (*buah keras*)	8
Coriander seeds (*ketumbar biji*)	1 Tbsp
Ground turmeric (*kunyit serbuk*)	1 tsp

Ingredients to be combined

Rice vinegar	1½ Tbsp
Dark soy sauce	1 dsp
Mustard	2 tsp

Method

- Season chicken with 1 tsp salt and set aside.
- Heat oil in a wok and lightly brown sliced ingredients.
- Add ground ingredients and fry for 5 minutes, then add mustard seeds and fry until fragrant.
- Add chicken and fry for a few minutes, then add water. Bring to the boil.
- Reduce heat, cover and simmer for 15 minutes, stirring occasionally, or until chicken is tender.
- Add combined ingredients and 1 tsp salt. Stir well and remove from heat.

Note: Debal or devil curry, as it is more popularly known, refers to hot curry.

Vindaloo Curry Powder

Preparation: 20 minutes

Ingredients

Dried chillies	600 g, stems removed
Cumin seeds (*jintan putih biji*)	600 g
Mustard seeds	300 g

Method

- Separately wash ingredients, then transfer to large flat trays or bamboo baskets.
- Dry spices in the sun for 2–3 days, turning occasionally to make sure ingredients are thoroughly dried.
- When well dried, send spices to the mill to be ground into a fine powder. Spread out and leave to cool before storing in airtight containers.
- The curry powder will keep for a few months.

Note: Use *vindaloo* curry powder for chicken, beef or pork vindaloo (page 57) and pada — salted or fresh fish pickle (page 50).

Pengat

Preparation: 10 minutes Cooking: 50 minutes Serves 6

Ingredients

Yam (taro)	700 g
Coconut cream	250 ml, squeezed from 1 grated coconut mixed with a little water
Coconut milk	750 ml, squeezed from same grated coconut with sufficient water added
Palm sugar (*gula Melaka*)	180 g, chopped
Sugar	90 g
Screwpine (*pandan*) leaves	4, washed and knotted
Bananas (*raja* variety)	4, medium

Method

- Peel yam and cut into thirds, then steam over rapidly boiling water for 25 minutes. Cut cooled yam into thick 5 x 2.5-cm pieces.
- Into a saucepan, put coconut milk, palm sugar, sugar and screwpine leaves. Simmer for 5 minutes, stirring gently, to melt sugar.
- Add in steamed yam and simmer gently for 15 minutes more.
- Meanwhile, peel and diagonally cut bananas into thick slices and add to coconut milk mixture.
- When mixture reaches the boil, add coconut cream.
- Serve hot or cold, for tea or as a sweet.

Laksa Lemak Melaka

Preparation: 25 minutes Cooking: 25 minutes

Ingredients

Cooking oil	150 ml
Large prawns (shrimps)	1 kg, unpeeled
Coconut milk	4 litres, squeezed from 3 grated coconuts with sufficient water added
Fish cakes	3, sliced
Salt	3 tsp
Fresh thick round rice (*laksa*) noodles	1.5 kg, or 2 packets of dried variety, scalded and drained

Ingredients to be ground

Shallots	600 g, peeled
Turmeric (*kunyit*)	5-cm knob, peeled
Dried chillies	40, soaked
Red chillies	6
Dried prawn (shrimp) paste (*belacan*)	5 x 4-cm piece
Candlenuts (*buah keras*)	10
Lemon grass (*serai*)	6 stalks
Galangal (*lengkuas*)	5 x 2.5-cm knob, peeled
Dried prawns (shrimps) (*hae be*)	60 g

Garnishing

Bean sprouts	600 g, tailed and scalded
Cucumbers	2, peeled and shredded
Mint leaves	2 sprigs

Method

- Heat oil in a wok. Fry ground ingredients until fragrant and oil separates.
- Add large prawns and stir-fry for 3 minutes or until prawns are cooked. Dish out prawns only and set aside to prevent overcooking.
- Pour in coconut milk and bring to the boil. Add fish cake slices.
- When liquid returns to the boil, return prawns. Add salt.
- To serve, put some noodles into individual serving bowls, then top with a little of each garnishing ingredient. Ladle gravy, with prawns and fish cake slices, over.

Popiah

Preparation: (filling and garnishing) 2 hours; (egg skins) 1 hour 15 minutes
Makes approximately 48–50 medium-size rolls

Ingredients

Egg skins*	1 recipe
Chinese lettuce	2 bunches, leaves separated
Red chillies	20, ground
Garlic	3 whole pods, peeled and ground
Black sweetened soy sauce (*tee cheo*)	
Bean sprouts	600 g, tailed and scalded
Cucumber	1, large, peeled if desired and finely shredded
Filling**	1 recipe (page 70)
Small prawns (shrimps)	300 g, peeled and steamed
Eggs	5, made into thin omelettes with 1/4 tsp each of salt and ground white pepper added, then finely sliced
Crabs	4, medium, steamed until cooked and meat extracted
Roasted skinned peanuts	300 g, ground
Shallots	300 g, peeled, sliced and crisp-fried

Method

- To assemble a *popiah* roll, put an egg skin on a plate and place a piece of lettuce on top, just below the centre.
- Spread on desired amounts of ground chillies and garlic, as well as black sweetened soy sauce. Top with bean sprouts and cucumber shreds.
- Drain about 2 Tbsp filling of gravy and place on top, then add on a few prawns, omelette strips and some crabmeat. Sprinkle on ground peanuts and crisp-fried shallot slices.
- Fold lower edge of egg skin over ingredients, then fold in left and right edges. Roll up Swiss-roll style.

*Egg Skins

Eggs	10
Water	2.125 litres
Plain (all-purpose) flour	600 g
Salt	$^1/_2$ tsp
Cooking oil for greasing	

Method

- Into a bowl, crack eggs and lightly beat with a fork. Gradually stir in water, then set aside.
- Into a second bowl, sift flour. Gradually add in egg mixture together with salt. Blend well.
- Strain mixture to remove lumps. Leave for 20 minutes.
- Lightly grease a 25-cm non-stick pan with a brush, then heat.
- Pour on a ladleful (about 3 Tbsp) of batter or enough to thinly spread over base. Cook over very low heat for 2 minutes or until pancake leaves side of pan.
- Remove and place on a flat dish. Repeat process, stacking cooked egg skins, until batter is used up.

**Filling

Chicken meat or pork belly	600 g, cut into thin strips
Small prawns (shrimps)	600 g, peeled and shells reserved for stock
Salt	as needed
Water	2.25 litres
Cooking oil	7 Tbsp
Garlic	3 whole pods, peeled and minced
Preserved soy beans (*tau cheo*)	5 Tbsp, lightly ground
Yam bean (*bangkuang*)	2 kg, peeled and shredded
Bamboo shoots	3 cans (each 552 g), drained and shredded
Firm bean curd (*tau kwa*)	10 pieces, cut into strips and fried

Method

- Separately season meat strips and prawns with 1 tsp salt each and set aside.
- Boil prawn shells in water for 5–10 minutes for stock. Strain stock and discard shells.
- Heat oil in a wok and lightly brown garlic. Add prawn stock and bring to the boil, then add yam beans and bamboo shoots.
- When liquid returns to the boil, add meat and simmer gently for 1 hour 30 minutes. Alternatively, pressure cook for 30 minutes.
- Add bean curd, prawns and salt to taste. Simmer for 10 minutes more.
- This filling may be prepared a day early, kept refrigerated and reheated before use.

Note: Prepare garnishing ingredients — ground chillies and garlic, scalded bean sprouts, cucumber shreds, steamed prawns, omelette shreds, crabmeat, ground peanuts and crisp-fried shallot slices — while cooking filling. To cut preparation time, crabmeat can be extracted a day ahead and frozen. Roasted ground peanuts and crisp-fried shallot slices can also be prepared well ahead and kept in airtight containers.

To make smooth egg skins, pan has to be just hot to set skin. If it is too hot, skin will turn out perforated.

Kuih Buah Melaka

Preparation: 20 minutes Cooking: 10 minutes Makes 38–40

Ingredients

Glutinous rice flour	240 g
Palm sugar (*gula Melaka*)	120 g, cut into small pieces
Skinned coconut	1/2, grated, mixed with a pinch of salt

Ingredients to be combined

Boiling water	190 ml
Screwpine (*pandan*) juice	1 Tbsp
Green food colouring	a few drops

Method

- Into a bowl, sift glutinous rice flour. Add combined ingredients and mix well, kneading into a firm lump of dough.
- Form marble-size balls from dough. Lightly flatten each ball and fill with 1–2 pieces of palm sugar. Press edges together and reshape into small balls.
- Half fill a saucepan with water and bring to the boil. Lower in glutinous rice balls, a few at a time.
- When cooked, glutinous rice balls will rise to the surface. Drain with a perforated ladle and roll them in grated coconut.

Note: Kuih buah melaka is also commonly known as kuih onde-onde. To obtain screwpine juice, pound 5–6 leaves with a little water using a mortar and pestle or blend in a blender (food processor). Press out juice and strain.

Bolu Koku (Coconut Sponge Cake)

Preparation: 20 minutes Baking: 50 minutes

Ingredients

Plain (all-purpose) flour	240 g
Ground cinnamon (*kayu manis serbuk*)	1/4 tsp
Eggs	6, large
Castor (superfine) sugar	300 g
Vanilla essence (extract)	1 tsp
Grated skinned coconut	240 g, finely ground
Salt	a pinch

Method

- Sift flour and ground cinnamon together. Set aside.
- Whisk eggs, sugar and vanilla essence until light and fluffy. Gradually add in sifted flour, then stir in ground coconut and salt.
- Pour batter into a greased 22-cm tube pan and bake in an oven preheated to 175°F/350°F for 50 minutes until top is golden brown.

Ayam Sioh (Tamarind Chicken)

Preparation: 15 minutes Cooking: 40 minutes

Ingredients

Chicken	1, about 1.5 kg, cut into 8 large pieces
Cooking oil	6 Tbsp

Tamarind Sauce

Tamarind pulp (*asam Jawa*)	360 g, mixed with 815 ml water and strained
Rice vinegar	1 1/2 Tbsp
Dark soy sauce	2 Tbsp
Sugar	10 Tbsp
Salt	2 tsp
Ground coriander (*ketumbar serbuk*)	3 Tbsp, made by pounding coriander that has been dry-fried until fragrant

Ingredients to be ground

Shallots	12, peeled
Garlic	3 cloves, peeled

Method

- In a mixing bowl, combine all sauce and ground ingredients. Mix in chicken pieces and leave to marinate overnight in the refrigerator.
- On cooking day, pour tamarind sauce into a pot and bring to a slow boil.
- Add chicken pieces and cook over moderate heat for 20 minutes or until chicken is tender.
- Remove chicken pieces and drain in a colander. Continue cooking sauce, stirring frequently, until thick. Remove from heat.
- Heat oil in a wok until hot. Fry chicken pieces for a few minutes or until brown.
- Arrange on a dish and pour thick sauce over.
- Serve hot or cold.

Negeri Sembilan

The name Negeri Sembilan, literally "nine states", alludes to the loose federation formed by Malay chiefs before they were united under British rule. Seremban, the state capital, with its narrow streets and backlanes, is typical of many of the towns that grew from the tin-mining centres many years ago. Travelling through, one cannot help noticing the distinctive Minangkabau influence, so evidently reflected in the style of houses with roofs that sweep to two buffalo horn-like peaks.

The region's Malay food is mostly burning hot, with a generous use of bird's eye chillies to give that extra kick. Well-made *rendang* dishes — especially the Rendang Rembau — though time-consuming to prepare, are unsurpassed in taste and flavour.

A pleasant 32-km drive from Seremban will take you into the heart of Port Dickson, a cosy, spruce and orderly seaside resort with friendly people and little traffic. That is until weekend visitors from nearby Kuala Lumpur and surrounding cities descend on the town in search of brief respite from urban life. Port Dickson has, besides the serenity and solitude of golden beaches, lots more attractions, food being no exception. Like most seaside resorts in Malaysia, seafood is readily available at food stalls and restaurants alike, in and around town. They are hardly cheap but the freshness is wonderful. For noodle lovers, Port Dickson boasts several specialties like Lor Mee, Sang Meen and Fried Mee Sua.

Rendang Ayam Negeri Sembilan

Preparation: 20 minutes   Cooking: 45 minutes

Ingredients

Chicken	1, about 1.5 kg, cut into bite-size pieces
Salt	as needed
Shallots	12, peeled and sliced
Garlic	6 cloves, peeled and sliced
Lemon grass (*serai*)	2 stalks, lightly crushed
Coconut cream	1 litre, squeezed from $1\frac{1}{2}$ grated coconuts with a little water added
Turmeric leaves (*daun kunyit*)	2
Grated skinned coconut	4 Tbsp, for *kerisik* (page 11)

Ingredients to be ground

Dried chillies	20, soaked
Bird's eye chillies (*cili padi*)	20
Ginger	2.5-cm knob, peeled
Galangal (*lengkuas*)	2.5-cm knob, peeled

Method

- Into a mixing bowl, put chicken, 1 tsp salt, shallots, garlic, lemon grass and ground ingredients. Mix well and leave for 30 minutes.
- Transfer marinated meat to a pot and add coconut cream. Bring to a slow boil.
- Add turmeric leaves and simmer gently, stirring constantly, until gravy is thick.
- Stir in *kerisik* and salt to taste, then simmer until chicken is tender and very little gravy remains.

Ikan Sembilang Masak Lemak Cili Padi

Preparation: 10 minutes Cooking: 15 minutes

Ingredients

Catfish (*ikan keli*)	450 g, cut into 5-cm thick slices
Salt	as needed
Turmeric leaf (*daun kunyit*)	1, torn through lengthways to get full fragrance
Dried sour fruit (*asam gelugur*)	2 pieces
Coconut cream	250 ml, squeezed from 1 grated coconut with a little water added
Coconut milk	500 ml, squeezed from same grated coconut with sufficient water added

Ingredients to be ground

Bird's eye chillies (*cili padi*)	20
Ginger	2.5-cm knob, peeled
Turmeric (*kunyit*)	2.5-cm knob, peeled
Shallots	7, peeled
Garlic	2 cloves, peeled

Method

- Rub fish with 1 tsp salt and leave for 15 minutes.
- Into a pot, put ground ingredients, turmeric leaf, dried sour fruit and coconut milk. Bring to a slow boil, stirring frequently.
- Add fish and simmer for 12 minutes or until gravy is thick. Add coconut cream and salt to taste.
- Serve with white rice.

Udang Goreng Cili Padi

Preparation: 10 minutes Cooking: 8 minutes

Ingredients

Prawns (shrimps)	12, medium-large, feelers and legs trimmed
Salt	as needed
Sugar	1/2 tsp
Cooking oil	2 Tbsp
Ground turmeric (*kunyit serbuk*)	1/2 tsp
Onions	3, peeled and sliced
Tamarind pulp (*asam Jawa*)	2 rounded (heaped) tsp, mixed with 65 ml water and strained
Red chilli	1, seeded and sliced

Ingredients to be ground

Bird's eye chillies (*cili padi*)	30
Turmeric (*kunyit*)	2.5-cm knob, peeled
Garlic	3 cloves, peeled

Method

- Season prawns with 1 tsp salt and sugar. Leave for 15 minutes.
- Heat oil in a wok. Fry ground ingredients and ground turmeric for 1 minute.
- Add onions and fry until transparent and fragrant, then add tamarind juice and bring to the boil.
- Add prawns and stir-fry for 2 minutes, then cover wok and allow to cook for 3 minutes.
- Uncover and add salt to taste. Add chilli slices last.
- Serve hot with rice.

Daging Masak Cili Padi

Preparation: 15 minutes Cooking: 40 minutes

Ingredients

Beef	600 g
Coconut milk	1.25 litres, squeezed from 1 1/2 grated coconuts with sufficient water added
Grated skinned coconut	2 rounded (heaped) Tbsp, for *kerisik* (page 11)
Salt	1 1/2 tsp or to taste

Ingredients to be ground

Bird's eye chillies (*cili padi*)	30
Turmeric (*kunyit*)	2.5-cm knob, peeled
Ginger	2.5-cm knob, peeled
Galangal (*lengkuas*)	1.25-cm knob, peeled
Shallots	12, peeled
Garlic	6 cloves, peeled
Lemon grass (*serai*)	2 stalks, sliced

Method

- Score meat before cutting into thin 4-cm slices.
- Into a pot, put meat, ground ingredients and coconut milk.
- Bring to the boil, then simmer gently for 30 minutes or until meat is tender.
- Add *kerisik* and salt to taste. Simmer for 5–10 minutes more or until gravy is thick.

Rendang Minangkabau

Preparation: 20 minutes Cooking: 1 hour 30 minutes

Ingredients

Beef	1 kg
Skinned coconuts	2, grated
Lemon grass (*serai*)	2 stalks, lightly crushed
Dried sour fruit (*asam gelugur*)	1 piece
Salt	2 tsp or to taste
Cooking oil	3 Tbsp

Ingredients to be ground

Dried chillies	25, soaked
Bird's eye chillies (*cili padi*)	10
Galangal (*lengkuas*)	2.5-cm knob, peeled
Ginger	2.5-cm knob, peeled
Turmeric (*kunyit*)	2.5-cm knob, peeled
Lemon grass (*serai*)	2 stalks
Shallots	15, peeled
Garlic	10 cloves, peeled

Ingredients to be sliced

Shallots	8, peeled
Garlic	4 cloves, peeled

Method

- Cut beef into 0.6-cm thick slices. Set aside.
- Reserve 4 Tbsp grated coconut for *kerisik* (page 11). With sufficient water added, squeeze remaining coconut for 1.5 litres coconut milk.
- Into a pot, put beef slices and ground ingredients. Mix well and leave to marinate for 15 minutes.
- Pour in coconut milk and bring to a slow boil. Then, add lemon grass and dried sour fruit. Simmer over low heat, stirring frequently, until gravy is quite thick.
- Add *kerisik* and continue simmering, stirring all the time, until meat is tender and gravy thick. Stir in salt to taste.
- Separately heat up oil in a saucepan. Brown sliced ingredients, then add to *rendang*.

Fried Mee Sua

Preparation: 30 minutes Cooking: 15 minutes Serves 5

Ingredients

Fine rice vermicelli (*mee sua*)	300 g, left unwashed
Cooking oil	as needed
Bean sprouts	450 g, tailed
Water	1.5 litres
Shallots	5, peeled and sliced
Garlic	4 cloves, peeled and minced
Chicken or pork	150 g, cut into strips
Small prawns (shrimps)	300 g, peeled
Salt	1 tsp
Ground white pepper	1 tsp
Anchovy (*ikan bilis*) or chicken stock	750 ml
Chinese flowering cabbage (*chye sim*)	4 stalks, cut into 5-cm lengths
Light soy sauce	2 Tbsp
Spring onions (scallions)	2, cut into 2.5-cm lengths
Coriander leaves (cilantro)	1 sprig, cut into 2.5-cm lengths
Red chillies	3–4, sliced and combined with 2 Tbsp light soy sauce

Method

- Deep-fry vermicelli, a bundle at a time, in hot oil until light golden, turning over quickly with chopsticks. Vermicelli will sizzle in hot oil; remove as soon as sizzling stops, takes about 15 seconds. Drain in a colander.
- Remove oil from wok, leaving behind about 3 Tbsp. Add bean sprouts and fry for 1 minute. Dish out and set aside.
- Pour water into wok and bring to the boil. Add fried vermicelli and cook for 1–2 minutes or until soft. Immediately pour vermicelli into a colander and drain well.
- Heat 3 Tbsp oil in a clean wok and brown shallots and garlic. Add meat and stir-fry for 2 minutes, then add prawns, salt and pepper. When cooked, dish out and set aside.
- Pour stock into wok and bring to the boil. Add Chinese flowering cabbage, stems before leaves, then add light soy sauce. Cook for 1 minute.
- Return vermicelli, bean sprouts, meat and prawns to wok and mix well. Then, add spring onions and coriander. Serve hot with chilli slices in light soy sauce.

Lor Mee

Preparation: 30 minutes Cooking: 15 minutes Serves 6

Ingredients

Chicken or pork	300 g, cut into strips
Small prawns (shrimps)	450 g, peeled
Squid	300 g, small–medium, cleaned
Salt	as needed
Ground white pepper	1 1/2 tsp
Light soy sauce	3 tsp
Cooking oil	3 Tbsp
Shallots	5, peeled and sliced
Garlic	5 cloves, peeled and minced
Anchovy (*ikan bilis*) or fresh chicken stock	1.75 litres
Carrot	1, cut into 5-cm strips
Chinese (napa) cabbage	4 leaves, cut into 1.25-cm strips
Light soy sauce	2 dsp
Dark soy sauce	1/2 tsp
Fish balls	12
Fresh yellow (Hokkien) noodles	1 kg
Black vinegar	4 Tbsp
Cornflour (cornstarch)	3 Tbsp, mixed with 125 ml water to make thickener
Eggs	2, lightly beaten
Spring onions (scallions)	2, chopped
Coriander (cilantro)	2 sprigs, chopped
Red chillies	3–4, sliced, combined with 2 Tbsp light soy sauce

Method

- Separately season meat, prawns and squid, each with 1/2 tsp salt, 1/2 tsp pepper and 1 tsp light soy sauce.
- Heat oil in a wok and brown shallots and garlic. Add chicken or pork and stir-fry for 2 minutes, then add prawns and squids. Stir-fry until just cooked. Dish out and keep aside.
- Pour stock into wok and bring to the boil. Add carrot and cabbage, soy sauces and fish balls. Simmer for 5 minutes.
- Add noodles and bring to a slow boil over moderate heat. Stir in vinegar, 1 tsp salt and thickener.
- Drizzle in beaten eggs over boiling gravy, stirring gently. Lastly, add spring onions and coriander.
- Serve hot with chilli slices in light soy sauce or *sambal belacan* (page 120).

Sang Meen

Preparation: 20 minutes Cooking: 15 minutes Serves 3

Ingredients

Fresh egg (wonton) noodles	300 g
Cooking oil	1 Tbsp
Sesame oil	1 tsp
Red chillies	3–4, sliced and combined with 2 Tbsp light soy sauce

Sauce

Chicken or pork	150 g, cut into strips
Small prawns (shrimps)	240 g, peeled
Squid	120 g, small–medium, cut into 1.25-cm pieces
Salt	1 1/2 tsp
Sesame oil	1 1/2 tsp
Ground white pepper	
Cooking oil	2 Tbsp
Garlic	3 cloves, peeled and minced
Anchovy (*ikan bilis*) or fresh chicken stock	500 ml
Chinese (napa) cabbage	1 leaf, cut into 0.6-cm strips
Chinese flowering cabbage (*chye sim*)	2–3 stalks, leaves and stems separated then cut into 5-cm lengths
Cornflour (cornstarch)	1 1/2 Tbsp, mixed with 65 ml water or stock to make thickener

Seasoning (combined)

Light soy sauce	1/2 Tbsp
Salt	1/2 tsp

Method

- Prepare noodles. Half fill a saucepan with water and bring to a rapid boil. Scald noodles for under 1 minute. Drain with a large wire-mesh ladle and immediately dip into a basin of cool water for a few seconds.
- Rescald noodles in boiling water for a few seconds before draining well and transferring to a deep dish. Mix in 1 Tbsp oil and 1 tsp sesame oil, then set aside.
- Prepare sauce. Separately season meat, prawns and squids, each with 1/2 tsp salt, 1/2 tsp sesame oil and a dash of pepper. Set aside, preferably for 15 minutes.
- Heat 2 Tbsp oil in a wok and brown garlic. Put in meat and stir-fry over high heat for 1 minute. Add prawns, then squid. Stir-fry until cooked. Dish out and leave aside.
- Pour stock into wok, add combined seasoning ingredients and bring to a rapid boil. Add Chinese cabbage and flowering cabbage, stems before leaves.
- When vegetables are just cooked, return meat, prawns and squids to wok. Allow liquid to return to the boil before stirring in thickener.
- Pour boiling hot sauce over noodles and serve immediately with combined chilli slices and light soy sauce.

Rendang Rembau

Preparation: 30 minutes   Cooking: 2 hours

Ingredients

Beef	1 kg, cut into 5-cm slices
Lemon grass (*serai*)	3 stalks, crushed
Shallots	12, peeled and sliced
Garlic	5 cloves, peeled and sliced
Grated skinned coconut	1 cup, for *kerisik* (page 11), coarsely ground
Water	750 ml
Coconut milk	750 ml, squeezed from 1 1/2 grated coconuts with sufficient water added
Salt	2 tsp
Cooking oil	3 Tbsp

Ingredients to be coarsely ground

Coriander (*ketumbar biji*)	1 cup, roasted
Black peppercorns	1 Tbsp, toasted

Ingredients to be finely ground

Dried chillies	30, soaked
Turmeric (*kunyit*)	2.5-cm knob, peeled
Ginger	2.5-cm knob, peeled
Galangal (*lengkuas*)	3 slices, peeled

Method

- In a mixing bowl, combine both lots of ground ingredients. Mix in beef slices and leave for 15 minutes.
- In a wok, combine seasoned beef, lemon grass, shallots, garlic, *kerisik* and water.
- Bring to the boil, then reduce heat and cook for 40 minutes, stirring occasionally.
- Add coconut milk and return to the boil, then simmer over low heat for 40 minutes, stirring continuously to ensure mixture does not stick to wok.
- When meat appears oily and dish is almost dry, reduce heat further. Add salt and oil and continue stirring for 20–25 minutes or until beef is dark brown and truly dry.

Note: Coriander seeds and black peppercorns can be placed in an oven preheated to 175°C/350°F for 20–25 minutes, stirring occasionally for even toasting, or pan-fried over medium heat for about 5 minutes or until fragrant. Wash coriander in lots of water before toasting. You'll be amazed to find the great amount of grit settling at the bottom of the container. To save time, coriander, peppercorns and *kerisik* can be milled dry.

Rendang rembau is dry and looks dark brown. It tastes deliciously different and is almost crisp out of the pan. It can be stored for a couple of weeks.

Sambal Tempoyak Petai

Preparation: 35 minutes Cooking: 15 minutes

Ingredients

Cooking oil	2 Tbsp
Dried anchovies (*ikan bilis*)	45 g, heads and entrails discarded
Coconut milk	565 ml, squeezed from 1 grated coconut with sufficient water added
Onions	2, peeled and sliced
Fermented durian (*tempoyak*)	3 Tbsp (page 146)
Stink beans (*petai*)	6–8 pods
Salt	1/2 tsp or to taste

Ingredients to be ground

Red chillies	20
Bird's eye chillies (*cili padi*)	20
Lemon grass (*serai*)	2 stalks, sliced
Turmeric (*kunyit*)	2.5-cm knob, peeled

Ingredients to be finely sliced

Turmeric leaves (*daun kunyit*)	4
Tender tapioca leaves	10
Young pumpkin leaves	10

Method

- Heat oil in a cooking pot and lightly brown anchovies.
- Pour in coconut milk, then add onions, ground ingredients and fermented durian. Bring to a slow boil, stirring at the same time.
- Add finely sliced leaves and simmer over low heat for 10 minutes.
- Meanwhile, extract stink beans from pods and peel off hard skins.
- Add beans and salt to taste and simmer for 5 minutes more or until gravy thickens.

Note: *Tempoyak* goes very well with rice. For those not too familiar with the dish, it may taste unusual, but it is not difficult to acquire a liking for it.

Sambal Tempoyak

Preparation: 10 minutes Cooking: 15 minutes

Ingredients

Fermented durian (*tempoyak*)	4 Tbsp (page 146)
Pure coconut cream (*pati santan*)	squeezed from 1 grated coconut
Dried anchovies (*ikan bilis*)	30 g, heads and entrails discarded
Lemon grass (*serai*)	5 stalks, ground
Salt	to taste

Ingredients to be ground

Bird's eye chillies (*cili padi*)	30
Turmeric (*kunyit*)	2.5-cm knob, peeled

Method

- Into a pot, put durian, coconut cream, anchovies and ground ingredients. Bring to a slow boil.
- Add lemon grass and salt to taste. Simmer gently for 10 minutes or until thick.
- Serve with white rice.

Lemang (Bamboo Glutinous Rice Rolls)

Preparation: 1 hour Cooking: 4 hours

Ingredients

Glutinous rice	4 kg
Coconuts	5, grated
Coarse salt	4 Tbsp
Green bamboo segments	24–26, each about 50-cm long and 5 cm in diameter
Young banana leaves	24–26, long edges trimmed, cut into pieces 55 cm in length and wide enough to line the interiors of bamboo segments
Firewood	

Method

- Wash glutinous rice thoroughly, then soak in water for 1 hour.
- Meanwhile, with sufficient water added, squeeze grated coconuts for enough coconut milk to cover rice for cooking.
- Drain rice and transfer to a large container. Add salt and enough coconut milk to cover rice completely. Mix well to dissolve salt.
- Line each segment of bamboo with a banana leaf, underside rolled in. This was traditionally done with a banana leaf stem that has been split along three-quarters of its length. Clip the long edge of banana leaf in between the split stem, then roll up tightly. Insert rolled leaf into hollow bamboo segment and carefully remove banana stem.
- Stamp bamboo segment on the ground to ensure that banana leaf goes right down to the bottom.
- Using a dessertspoon, fill four-fifths of lined bamboo segment with rice and just enough coconut milk to cover rice.
- Stamp filled bamboo segment on the ground twice to firmly pack rice. Fold and tuck in top end of banana leaf to seal in rice. Repeat until ingredients are used up.
- Start a fire. Arrange bamboo segments in a neat row, propped against a horizontally secured pole about 70 cm away from the fire. Cook for between 3 hours 30 minutes and 4 hours, turning segments frequently to prevent burning. While turning, stamp segments twice again to pack in rice.
- When rice is cooked, split the bamboo segments with a sharp knife. Cut glutinous rice rolls into 2.5-cm thick pieces. Serve with your favourite *rendang* dish.

Note: *Lemang* is a firm Hari Raya favourite and it is usually prepared by elders in the *kampung*, or rural village, where bamboo and firewood are readily available. It is so important with most *kampung* folk that wives would quarrel bitterly with their husbands if glutinous rice had not been purchased for this specialty in anticipation of Hari Raya celebrations.

Lemang will keep well for 3–4 days without refrigeration if the glutinous rice was thoroughly washed before cooking. In other words, the rice should have been washed in multiple changes of water, with the last of which emerging clear.

Dodol

Preparation: 15 minutes Cooking 2 hours 30 minutes

Ingredients

Glutinous rice flour	1 kg
Coconut milk	1.75 litres, squeezed from 4 grated coconuts with sufficient water added

Syrup

Palm sugar (*gula Melaka*)	700 g, chopped
Sugar	240 g
Water	250 ml
Screwpine (*pandan*) leaves	3, washed and knotted

Method

- Into a saucepan, put all syrup ingredients and cook until both sugars are completely dissolved. Set aside.
- Put glutinous rice flour into a bowl and blend with coconut milk until smooth. Strain mixture into a large non-stick pan.
- Cook mixture over low heat, stirring all the time with a wooden spoon, until mixture starts to thicken.
- Strain palm sugar syrup into flour mixture and continue stirring for 2 hours or until mixture turns into an oily lump of dark brown dough.
- Transfer dough to a *mengkuang* (screwpine mat) basket. If unavailable, divide dough into two 25 x 15-cm ungreased pyrex dishes.
- Smoothen surface with a plastic spatula and leave to cool completely, preferably overnight, before cutting.

Note: Different brands of store bought palm sugar vary in quality, which affects the colour of the *dodol*. Generally, the better the quality, the darker the brown.

Selangor

When one talks of Selangor, invariably the discussion drifts to Kuala Lumpur, formerly the state capital of Selangor. The new state capital is Shah Alam.

Kuala Lumpur, the capital city, throbs with vitality, and although more than a hundred years old, it is a melting pot of inhabitants from other states and towns in Malaysia. This is probably why it is a veritable gourmet's paradise, with some of the best cosmopolitan cuisines in the nation. The cluster of international hotels in the 'Golden Triangle' cater authentic Malay, Chinese and Indian, as well as international cuisines.

Malay food is a rich mixture of curries and hot chilli pastes (*sambal*) drawing from the north to south of Peninsular Malaysia, with some still waiting to be discovered. Even the most discerning of gourmets will find the range wide and enticing.

The variety of Chinese dishes to be encountered in Kuala Lumpur is amazing. Every provincial variety, cooked to perfection, is available here, be it Cantonese (Guangdong), Hokkien (Fujian), Hakka, Teochew (Chaozhou), Hainanese, Shanghainese, Peking (Beijing), Taiwanese or Szechuan (Sichuan).

First-class restaurants may be found throughout Kuala Lumpur and Selangor, but one should not ignore the food stalls that do a roaring trade catering to the local populace with favourites like Bak Kut Teh and the typically 'KL' Hokkien Mee.

Fish Head Curry

Preparation: 15 minutes   Cooking: 25 minutes

Ingredients

Fish head	1, about 1 kg
Salt	as needed
Cooking oil	5 Tbsp
Fish curry powder	30 g, mixed with 3 Tbsp water into a paste
Tamarind pulp (*asam Jawa*)	90 g, mixed with 250 ml water and strained
Coconut milk	750 ml, squeezed from 1 grated coconut with sufficient water added
Lady's fingers (okra)	10
Tomatoes	3, halved
Red chillies	5
Green chillies	5
Sugar	1 tsp

Ingredients to be ground

Dried chillies	25
Shallots	12, peeled
Garlic	2 cloves, peeled
Lemon grass (*serai*)	3 stalks, sliced
Galangal (*lengkuas*)	2.5-cm knob, peeled
Dried prawn (shrimp) paste (*belacan*)	2.5-cm square piece

Method

- Clean fish head thoroughly and rub with 1 tsp salt.
- Heat oil in a wok and fry ground ingredients for 3 minutes.
- Add curry powder paste and fry until fragrant and oil separates.
- Pour in tamarind juice and coconut milk. Bring to the boil, then reduce heat and simmer for 5 minutes.
- Add lady's fingers, then tomatoes and chillies. Simmer for 5 minutes.
- Stir in sugar and 1 1/2 tsp salt and lastly, lower in fish head. Cook for 10 minutes or until fish is done.
- Serve hot with white rice.

Stuffed Horse Mackerel

Preparation: 10 minutes Cooking: 8 minutes

Ingredients

Horse mackerels (*ikan cupak*)	3, large
Salt	1 1/2 tsp
Cooking oil	4 Tbsp
Lettuce	1 small head

Ingredients to be ground

Dried prawns (shrimps) (*hae be*)	90 g, washed and drained dry
Red chillies	6
Dried prawn (shrimp) paste (*belacan*)	2.5-cm square piece
Lemon grass (*serai*)	1 stalk
Shallots	8, peeled
Garlic	2 cloves, peeled

Method

- Wash and clean fish, then remove and discard hard outer skins. Make deep slits parallel to the backbone on both sides of each fish, taking care not to cut right through.
- Rub fish with salt, then smear ground ingredients into slits and cavities.
- Heat oil in a wok until hot. Cook fish for 3–4 minutes on each side. When well browned, remove and drain well.
- Serve hot on a bed of lettuce leaves.

Fish Slices with Cauliflower

Preparation: 20 minutes Cooking: 15 minutes

Ingredients

Threadfin (*ikan kurau/ senangin*)	600 g, central portion
Egg	1, lightly beaten
Cornflour (cornstarch)	1 tsp + 1 rounded (heaped) tsp, mixed with 1 Tbsp water to make thickener
Salt	as needed
Cooking oil for deep-frying	
Cauliflower	240 g, cut into pieces
Garlic	6 cloves, peeled and minced
Carrot	10 slices, peeled if desired and parboiled
Leek	1 stalk, green portion discarded, cut into 5-cm lengths
Canned button mushrooms	1/2 can (365 g), halved
Fresh chicken stock	190 ml
Sesame oil	1/4 tsp
Peas	1 Tbsp
Spring onion (scallion)	1, chopped

Ingredients to be combined

Rice wine	1 tsp
Light soy sauce	1 Tbsp
Oyster sauce	1/2 Tbsp
Dark soy sauce	1 tsp
Ground white pepper	1/4 tsp

Method

- Cut fish into 4 x 2.5 x 1.25-cm pieces, then mix with egg, cornflour and 1 tsp salt.
- Heat oil for deep-frying in a wok. Add cauliflower pieces and stir for 10 seconds. Remove and set aside.
- Add fish slices to wok and deep-fry for 1 minute, then dish out and set aside.
- Remove oil from wok, leaving behind about 1 Tbsp. Lightly brown garlic, then add fried cauliflower, carrot, leek and mushrooms. Fry for 2 minutes.
- Add combined ingredients, then fried fish. Pour in stock and bring to a quick boil.
- Add sesame oil, salt to taste, and peas. Stir in thickener and serve hot, garnished with spring onion.

Sweet and Sour Fish

Preparation: 10 minutes Cooking: 20 minutes

Ingredients

Garoupa (*ikan kerapu*)	600 g, 2 slits made across each side
Salt	1 1/2 tsp
Cornflour (cornstarch)	1 1/2 Tbsp
Cooking oil for deep-frying	

Sauce

Cooking oil	1 1/2 Tbsp
Garlic	4 cloves, peeled and minced
Onions	2, peeled and cut into wedges
Red chillies	2, cut into strips
Ginger	2 slices, peeled and cut into strips
Cucumber	1, soft portion removed and cut into wedges
Tomatoes	2, cut into wedges
Cornflour (cornstarch)	1 1/2 Tbsp, mixed with 2 Tbsp water to make thickener
Plum sauce	1/2 Tbsp

Ingredients to be combined

Water	500 ml
Tomato sauce (ketchup)	3 Tbsp
Chilli sauce	2 Tbsp
Sugar	1 Tbsp
Salt	1/2 tsp

Garnishing

Coriander leaves (cilantro)

Spring onion (scallion)

Method

- Rub fish with 1 1/2 tsp salt and 1 1/2 Tbsp cornflour.
- Heat oil for deep-frying in a wok until hot. Lower in fish and fry for 15 minutes or until fish is cooked and golden.
- Drain fish and place on an oval serving dish. Set aside.
- Prepare sauce. Heat oil in a wok and fry garlic, onions, chillies and ginger for 1 minute. Then, add combined ingredients.
- When liquid reaches the boil, put in cucumber, tomatoes and thickener. Lastly, stir in plum sauce.
- To serve, pour sauce over fish and garnish. Serve hot.

Shark's Fin Soup

Preparation: 20 minutes Cooking: 6 minutes

Ingredients

Crabs	600 g, preferably with roe, steamed, with meat and roe separately extracted
Eggs	2, lightly beaten with 2 Tbsp water
Corn oil	2 Tbsp
Rice wine	1 Tbsp
Fresh chicken stock	500 ml
Pre-prepared shark's fin	180 g, washed and drained
Salt	1 tsp
Light soy sauce	1 dsp
Ground white pepper	1/2 tsp
Cornflour (cornstarch)	2 Tbsp, mixed with 2 Tbsp water to make thickener
Corn oil	1 Tbsp

Method

- Mince crab roe and stir into beaten egg mixture. Set aside.
- Heat 2 Tbsp corn oil in a wok until hot. Add rice wine, then chicken stock and bring to the boil.
- Add shark's fin and stir well, then add salt, soy sauce, pepper and crabmeat.
- When liquid returns to the boil, add thickener and simmer over low heat. Gradually stir in beaten egg mixture and add 1 Tbsp corn oil.
- Serve immediately.

Fish Maws Topped with Prawns

Preparation: 25 minutes Steaming: 12 minutes Cooking: 5 minutes

Ingredients

Dried fish maws (*hee peow*)	75 g
Cooking oil	as needed
Alkaline water (*kan sui*)	1 tsp
Prawns (shrimps)	1 kg, peeled and minced
Egg whites	1 lightly beaten
Salt	1/2 tsp
Ground white pepper	1/4 tsp
Crab roe	
Rice wine	1 dsp
Crabmeat	240 g
Button mushrooms	8–10, sliced
Snow peas	10, or 90 g peas
Coriander leaves (cilantro) (optional)	

Sauce (combined)

Fresh chicken stock	250 ml
Salt	1/2 tsp
Ground white pepper	1/4 tsp
Cornflour (cornstarch)	1 tsp

Method

- Dry fish maws in the sun for 1 hour, then deep-fry until puffy.
- Soak fried maws in a basin of water until soft. Fish maws are light and tend to float, so be mindful to weigh them down.
- Cut soaked and softened fish maws into matchbox-size pieces; there should be about 24.
- Drain maw pieces well before mixing with alkaline water. Then, wash thoroughly with water, squeeze dry and set aside. Hard pieces, if any, should be discarded.
- Season prawn meat with 1 egg white, salt and pepper. Then, beat with a spoon until mixture is sticky.
- Spread a spoonful of prawn meat atop each fish bladder. Top with a little crab roe. If unavailable, substitute with a little minced carrot.
- With prepared fish maws on a serving dish, steam for 12 minutes.
- Heat 1 Tbsp oil in a wok. Add rice wine, then crabmeat, mushrooms and snow peas or peas. Stir-fry for 1–2 minutes.
- Add combined sauce ingredients and bring to the boil. As soon as liquid thickens, spoon half the sauce over steamed fish maws.
- Stir beaten egg white into remaining gravy. When it returns to the boil, pour over fish maws.
- Garnish with coriander, if desired. Serve hot.

Scrambled Eggs with Shark's Fin

Preparation: 15 minutes **Cooking:** 6 minutes

Ingredients

Pre-prepared shark's fin	180 g
Cooked crabmeat	180 g
Chicken	60 g, steamed or boiled until cooked and cut into strips
Eggs	6
Corn oil	1 Tbsp
Ground white pepper	1 tsp
Salt	1 tsp
Light soy sauce	1 dsp
Rice wine	1 dsp
Cooking oil	6 Tbsp
Bean sprouts	60 g, heads and tails pinched off
Spring onion (scallion)	1, cut into 2.5-cm lengths
Coriander leaves (cilantro)	2 sprigs
Chinese lettuce	1–2 bunches

Method

- Wash shark's fin and drain well.
- Into a mixing bowl, put shark's fin, crabmeat, chicken, eggs, 1 Tbsp corn oil, pepper, salt, soy sauce and rice wine. Mix well and set aside.
- Heat 1 Tbsp oil in a wok until very hot. Fry bean sprouts for 1 minute, then remove and set aside.
- Heat 1 Tbsp oil in the wok and pour in egg mixture. Scramble gently and at the same time, add remaining oil, a tablespoon at a time. When egg mixture is almost cooked, put in bean sprouts and spring onion. Stir-fry to mix well.
- Garnish with coriander. Serve hot with lettuce.

Prawn and Pineapple Curry

Preparation: 15 minutes Cooking: 15 minutes

Ingredients

Prawns (shrimps)	12, large
Cooking oil	3 Tbsp
Lemon grass (*serai*)	2 stalks, lightly crushed
Ripe pineapple	1/2, small, peeled and sliced
Coconut cream	250 ml, squeezed from 1 grated coconut with a little water added
Coconut milk	500 ml, squeezed from same grated coconut with sufficient water added
Salt	1 1/2 tsp

Ingredients to be ground

Red chillies	8
Shallots	15, peeled
Galangal (*lengkuas*)	5-cm knob, peeled
Turmeric (*kunyit*)	2.5-cm knob, peeled
Dried prawn (shrimp) paste (*belacan*)	2.5-cm square piece
Candlenuts (*buah keras*)	3

Method

- Wash prawns. Trim off feelers and legs. Leave unpeeled.
- Heat oil in a wok. Fry lemon grass and ground ingredients until fragrant and oil separates.
- Add pineapple slices, then coconut milk. Bring to a slow boil and simmer gently for 5 minutes.
- Put in prawns and simmer until almost cooked, then add coconut cream and salt. Simmer until prawns are thoroughly cooked.

Prawn Sambal

Preparation: 20 minutes Cooking: 20 minutes

Ingredients

Prawns (shrimps)	600 g, peeled and deveined
Salt	as needed
Cooking oil	4 Tbsp
Onions	2, peeled and sliced
Garlic	4 cloves, peeled and sliced
Tamarind pulp (*asam Jawa*)	1 rounded (heaped) tsp, mixed with 4 Tbsp water and strained
Tomatoes	2, cut into wedges
Pure coconut cream (*pati santan*)	250 ml, squeezed from 1 grated coconut

Ingredients to be ground

Dried chillies	10, soaked, or 2 tsp chilli powder
Red chillies	6
Turmeric (*kunyit*)	2.5-cm knob, peeled
Coriander seeds (*ketumbar biji*)	2 tsp
Cumin seeds (*jintan putih biji*)	1 tsp
Black peppercorns	6
Fenugreek seeds (*halba*)	1/2 tsp

Method

- Rub prawns with 1 tsp salt, then wash and drain in a colander.
- Heat oil in a wok. Lightly brown onions and garlic, takes 2–3 minutes.
- Add ground ingredients and fry until fragrant and oil separates.
- Add tamarind juice and tomatoes and simmer gently for 10 minutes.
- Add prawns, then coconut cream and salt to taste. Bring to the boil over low heat, stirring constantly, until prawns are cooked.
- Serve with white rice.

Plum Sauce Prawns

Preparation: 10 minutes Cooking: 8 minutes

Ingredients

Cooking oil	5 Tbsp
Prawns (shrimps)	600 g, large, feelers trimmed
Ginger	5-cm knob, peeled and chopped
Garlic	4 cloves, peeled and minced
Plum sauce	1 Tbsp
Coriander leaves (cilantro)	2 sprigs, chopped
Spring onions (scallions)	2, chopped

Seasoning (combined)

Dark soy sauce	1 dsp
Light soy sauce	1 dsp
Sugar	1 dsp
Salt	1 tsp

Method

- Heat oil in a wok until hot. Add prawns and fry for 2 minutes or until they turn red. Remove and drain.
- Remove oil from wok, leaving behind about 2 tablespoonfuls. Brown ginger and garlic, then return prawns to wok. Stir-fry.
- Add combined seasoning ingredients and stir-fry quickly until prawns are cooked through, then mix in all remaining ingredients.
- Dish out and serve hot.

Chilli Oyster Crabs

Preparation: 15 minutes   Cooking: 20 minutes

Ingredients

Crabs	3 kg
Cooking oil	175 ml
Ginger	60 g, peeled and cut into strips
Garlic	7 cloves, peeled and sliced
Shallots	7, peeled and sliced
Red chillies	10, seeded, and blended (processed) with 125 ml water
Eggs	5, lightly beaten
Spring onions (scallions)	6, cut into 5-cm lengths
Coriander leaves (cilantro)	2 sprigs, cut into 5-cm lengths

Sauce (combined)

Rice wine	3 Tbsp
Chilli sauce	3 Tbsp
Oyster sauce	4 Tbsp
Sugar	4 dsp
Light soy sauce	1 tsp
Sesame oil	1 tsp
Ground white pepper	$^1/_4$ tsp

Method

- Clean crabs. Dislocate pincers, then crack with a pestle. Trim legs and quarter each crab.
- Heat oil in a large wok. Stir-fry ginger, garlic and shallots until fragrant, then add ground chillies and fry for 2 minutes.
- Add crabs and stir briskly. Cover wok and leave to cook for 4–5 minutes. Uncover and stir briskly before adding combined sauce ingredients.
- When crabs are bright red and nearly cooked, pour in beaten eggs. Then, add spring onions, stirring to mix with sauce.
- Serve hot, garnished with coriander.

Crispy Prawn Fritters

Preparation: 15 minutes Cooking: 15 minutes

Ingredients

Prawns (shrimps)	600 g, large
Cooking oil for deep-frying	
Cucumber slices for garnishing	
Tomato slices for garnishing	

Seasoning

Bicarbonate of (baking) soda	1/2 tsp
Salt	1/2 tsp
Sugar	1 tsp
Egg white	1/2
Cornflour (cornstarch)	1 Tbsp
Cooking oil	1 dsp

Batter

Self-raising flour	120 g
Rice flour	240 g
Baking powder	1 1/2 tsp
Sugar	1/2 tsp
Salt	1/2 tsp
Water	375 ml
Tobasco sauce	1/2 tsp

Sweet-Sour Chilli Sauce (combined)

Chilli sauce	4 Tbsp
Tomato sauce (ketchup)	1 Tbsp
Kalamansi lime (*limau kesturi*) juice	squeezed from 5 limes
Plum sauce	2 Tbsp
Sugar	2 Tbsp
A1 sauce	1 dsp
Salt	1/4 tsp
Garlic	1 clove, peeled and ground

Method

- Peel prawns but leave tails intact. Devein, then wash and dry with a clean piece of cloth.
- Put prawns into a mixing bowl. Of seasoning ingredients, add bicarbonate of soda, salt and sugar. Mix well.
- Add to prawns all remaining seasoning ingredients. When well combined, leave for at least 30 minutes.
- Prepare batter. Sift flours and baking powder into a mixing bowl, then add sugar and salt.
- Make a well at the centre and gradually blend in water. Resulting batter should be smooth in consistency, slightly thick and not too runny. Stir in tobasco sauce.
- Heat oil for deep-frying in a wok. Dip prawns into batter and fry until golden brown. Drain on absorbent paper.
- Arrange fried prawns on a serving plate garnished with cucumber and tomato slices. Serve hot with sweet-sour chilli sauce.

Prawn Curry

Preparation: 10 minutes Cooking: 12–15 minutes

Ingredients

Prawns (shrimps)	12, large, unpeeled, feelers and legs trimmed
Cooking oil	3 Tbsp
Salt	1 1/2 tsp
Coconut cream	250 ml, squeezed from 1 grated coconut with a little water added
Coconut milk	500 ml, squeezed from the same grated coconut with sufficient water added

Ingredients to be ground

Red chillies	10
Shallots	12, peeled
Garlic	4 cloves, peeled
Lemon grass (*serai*)	2 stalks, sliced
Turmeric (*kunyit*)	2.5-cm knob, peeled
Galangal (*lengkuas*)	1.25-cm knob, peeled
Candlenuts (*buah keras*)	4

Method

- Into a mixing bowl, put prawns and ground ingredients. Mix well and leave to season for 30 minutes.
- Heat oil in a wok. Add seasoned prawns and fry for 3–4 minutes.
- Add salt and coconut milk and bring to the boil.
- Reduce heat and add coconut cream. Simmer, stirring frequently, until prawns are cooked.

Yim Kok Har (Fried Salted Prawns)

Preparation: 10 minutes Cooking: 5 minutes

Ingredients

Prawns (shrimps)	600 g, large, washed, feelers and legs trimmed but unpeeled
Water	750 ml
Salt	as needed
Five-spice powder	1 rounded (heaped) tsp
Egg white	1, lightly beaten
Ground white pepper	1/4 tsp
Cooking oil for deep-frying	

Ingredients to be sifted together

Cornflour (cornstarch)	2 Tbsp
Rice flour	1 Tbsp
Plain (all-purpose) flour	1 Tbsp
Five-spice powder	1/4 tsp
Ground white pepper	a pinch

Garnishing

Cucumber	1/2, peeled if desired and sliced
Tomato	1, sliced
Coriander leaves (cilantro)	

Method

- Put cleaned prawns into a bowl and add 750 ml or just enough water to cover prawns. Stir in 3 tsp salt and five-spice powder. Refrigerate for 2 hours.
- Drain and dry prawns with a clean tea towel, then mix with egg white, 1/2 tsp salt and pepper.
- With sifted ingredients already combined in a bowl, dip in prawns to coat thoroughly.
- Deep-fry coated prawns until golden brown. Serve garnished.

Note: Instead of dipping prawns into sifted flour mixture, prawns can be placed on a flat tray and have combined flour mixture carefully sifted over. Turn prawns over and sift on more flour mixture to coat completely.

Chinese Beef Steak

Preparation: 10 minutes Cooking: 15 minutes

Ingredients

Beef fillet steak	700 g
Cooking oil	3 Tbsp
Cornflour (cornstarch)	1 dsp, mixed with 2 Tbsp water to make thickener

Seasoning

Light soy sauce	2 tsp
Bicarbonate of (baking) soda	1 tsp
Salt	1/2 tsp
Ginger juice	1 dsp
Sugar	1 Tbsp
Cornflour (cornstarch)	1 Tbsp
Egg	1, lightly beaten

Sauce (combined)

Stock or water	125 ml
Light soy sauce	2 Tbsp
Dark soy sauce	1/2 Tbsp
Oyster sauce	1 Tbsp
Sugar	1 Tbsp
Sesame oil	1/2 tsp
Salt	1/4 tsp
Ground white pepper	1/4 tsp

Garnishing

Coriander leaves (cilantro)	as desired, cut into 5-cm lengths
Spring onions (scallions)	2, cut into 5-cm lengths
Red chilli	1, seeded and cut into strips

Method

- Cut fillet steak into 0.6-cm thick slices. Then, using the back of a cleaver, lightly score meat slices to tenderise.
- Into a mixing bowl, put beef and seasoning ingredients, adding beaten egg last. Mix well and leave for 3 hours.
- Heat oil in a wok until hot. Fry beef slices until slightly brown on both sides.
- Remove and arrange on a dish.
- Pour combined sauce ingredients into the wok. Bring to the boil, then stir in thickener.
- When liquid is thickened, remove from heat and pour sauce over beef.
- Garnish and serve hot.

Peh Pa Ngap (Roasted Duck with Plum Sauce)

Preparation: 5 minutes Steaming: 1 hour Cooking: 25 minutes

Ingredients

Pre-roasted duck	1
Cooking oil	as needed
Sesame seeds	1 Tbsp, roasted
Coriander leaves (cilantro)	

Sauce (combined)

Tomato sauce (ketchup)	3 Tbsp
Chilli sauce	1 Tbsp
Plum sauce	1 Tbsp
Sugar	$2^1/_2$ dsp
Salt	$^1/_2$ tsp
Sesame oil	2 tsp
A1 sauce	2 Tbsp
Worcestershire sauce	1 Tbsp
Hot water	5 Tbsp
Cornflour (cornstarch)	1 tsp

Method

- Prepare a steamer for use. When water is rapidly boiling, put in duck and steam for 1 hour. If preferred, duck can be steamed the night before.
- Using a sharp cleaver, cut along breast of steamed duck so that it can lie flat on a plate, splayed.
- Heat sufficient oil for deep-frying in a wok until hot. Fry duck, turning over occasionally, for 15–20 minutes or until skin is crisp and golden brown.
- Cut fried duck into serving-size pieces and neatly arrange them on a dish.
- Heat 4 Tbsp oil in a clean wok and add combined sauce ingredients. When liquid thickens, spoon it over duck pieces.
- Sprinkle on roasted sesame seeds and serve hot, garnished with coriander.

Crispy Skin Chicken

Preparation: 10 minutes Cooking: 25 minutes

Ingredients

Chicken	1, about 1.5 kg
Salt	as needed
Cinnamon (*kayu manis*)	3 sticks, each 7.5-cm long
Kalamansi lime (*limau kesturi*) juice	squeezed from 10 limes, strained
Malt sugar (*mak ngar tong*)	2 Tbsp
Cooking oil for deep-frying	

Garnishing

Cucumber slices
Tomato slices
Prawn (shrimp) crackers

Method

- Clean chicken thoroughly. Remove pancreas and cut off feet. Discard both.
- Break chicken's thigh bone joints and carefully remove thigh bones from the inside with the help of a small knife. Leave drumstick bones intact.
- Rub inside of chicken with 1 Tbsp salt. Position cinnamon sticks horizontally across chest cavity. Set aside.
- Ensure that a wok is greaseless before use. Then, half fill with water and bring to the boil. Meanwhile, firmly tie chicken's neck with some strong string.
- When water is rapidly boiling, position chicken just above liquid surface, holding it by the string. Scald chicken several times by ladling boiling water over.
- Set scalded chicken aside and discard boiling water. Wash wok thoroughly so that it is again greaseless.
- Half fill clean wok with water and bring to the boil. Add strained lime juice, then stir in malt sugar and 1 tsp salt.
- When malt sugar is completely dissolved, lower in chicken and turn quickly. Remove and hang in the sun to dry for 5 hours.
- Deep-fry prepared chicken for 15 minutes or until golden brown. If chicken browns too quickly, reduce heat. Should air bubbles appear on chicken skin, prick with a skewer to remove.
- Cut fried chicken into serving-size pieces, then garnish and serve hot.

Note: Pick a chicken with perfect skin, without a tear or slit, for this recipe.

Steamed Chicken with Glutinous Rice

Preparation: 30 minutes   Cooking: 15 minutes   Steaming: 90 minutes

Ingredients

Chicken	1, about 1.5 kg, cleaned
Glutinous rice	1 kg, washed and drained
Cooking oil	5 Tbsp
Dried Chinese mushrooms	60 g, soaked to soften, stems discarded and cut into strips
Shallots	8, peeled and sliced
Salt	2 tsp
Dark soy sauce	1 tsp
Five-spice powder	1 rounded (heaped) tsp
Water	1 litre

Seasoning

Oyster sauce	4 Tbsp
Rice wine	2 tsp
Dark soy sauce	1 tsp
Light soy sauce	2 tsp
Ginger juice	2 tsp
Sesame oil	1 tsp
Sugar	1 tsp
Ground white pepper	1/2 tsp
Cornflour (cornstarch)	1 rounded (heaped) tsp

Garnishing

Red chillies	2, seeded and sliced
Spring onions (scallions)	2, chopped
Coriander leaves (cilantro)	4 sprigs, cut into 2.5-cm lengths

Method

- Debone chicken and cut into 1.25-cm thick slices. Mix chicken and seasoning ingredients in a bowl. Leave for at least 1 hour.
- Steam glutinous rice for 45 minutes and set aside.
- Heat oil in a wok. Fry mushrooms for 1–2 minutes, drain and set aside. In the same oil, lightly brown shallots. Add glutinous rice, salt, dark soy sauce and five-spice powder. Fry for 1 minute before adding water. Mix well, cover and simmer gently for 5–10 minutes. Remove from heat.
- Grease 12 medium rice bowls. Put some mushrooms and chicken into each bowl. Top with glutinous rice to fill three-quarters of bowl, pressing down with the back of a spoon.
- Steam filled bowls over rapidly boiling water for 45 minutes.
- To serve, turn out onto a small dish, garnish and serve hot.

Steamed Chicken Wings

Preparation: 10 minutes   Steaming: 12 minutes

Ingredients

Chicken wings	6 pairs, cut at the joints
Cooking oil	1/2 Tbsp
Dried Chinese mushrooms	2, soaked to soften, stems discarded and sliced
Red chillies	2, seeded and sliced
Coriander leaves (cilantro)	1 sprig, chopped
Spring onion (scallion)	1, chopped

Seasoning

Light soy sauce	1 Tbsp
Oyster sauce	1 Tbsp
Cornflour (cornstarch)	2 tsp
Sugar	1 tsp
Dark soy sauce	1 tsp
Salt	1/2 tsp
Ground white pepper	1/4 tsp
Ginger	2.5-cm knob, peeled and minced

Method

- Wash and dry chicken wings thoroughly.
- Into a mixing bowl, put chicken wings, seasoning ingredients and 1 Tbsp oil. Mix well and leave for 1 hour.
- Transfer chicken to a heatproof dish. Sprinkle on mushroom and chilli slices.
- Steam over rapidly boiling water for 12 minutes.
- Serve hot, sprinkled with chopped coriander and spring onion.

Chicken Rendang

Preparation: 15 minutes Cooking: 40 minutes

Ingredients

Chicken	1, about 1.5 kg, cut into bite-size pieces
Salt	as needed
Black peppercorns	1 tsp, ground
Cooking oil	100 ml
Lemon grass (*serai*)	3 stalks, lightly crushed
Coconut milk	500 ml, squeezed from 1 grated coconut with sufficient water added

Ingredients to be ground

Dried chillies	15
Onions	150 g, peeled
Shallots	150 g, peeled
Garlic	1 whole pod, peeled
Red chillies	12
Turmeric (*kunyit*)	4-cm knob, peeled

Method

- Season chicken pieces with 1 tsp salt and ground black peppercorns. Leave for 30 minutes.
- Heat oil in a wok until hot. Fry seasoned chicken for 5 minutes or until lightly browned. Drain and remove chicken with a perforated ladle, leaving oil behind.
- To heated oil, add ground ingredients and lemon grass. Fry until fragrant and oil separates.
- Reduce heat, pour in coconut milk and bring to a slow boil. Return chicken pieces to wok and add 1 tsp salt. Simmer until chicken is tender and gravy thick.

Spicy Mutton Soup

Preparation: 10 minutes Cooking: 2 hours

Ingredients

Mutton	1 kg, fatty streaks removed, cut into 2.5-cm cubes
Water	2.5 litres
Salt	2 tsp

Spices

Cinnamon (*kayu manis*)	5-cm stick
Cloves (*bunga cengkih*)	8
Star anise (*bunga lawang*)	2 whole
White peppercorns	1 tsp
Coriander seeds (*ketumbar biji*)	1/2 tsp
Fennel seeds (*jintan manis biji*)	1/2 tsp
Cumin seeds (*jintan putih biji*)	1/2 tsp

Garnishing

Shallots	8, peeled, sliced and crisp-fried
Garlic	3 cloves, peeled, sliced and crisp-fried
Spring onions (scallions)	2, chopped

Method

- Into a pot, put mutton cubes and water. Bring to the boil.
- Lightly crush spices before wrapping with a piece of clean, muslin cloth. To secure, tie ends together with string.
- Drop spice bag into boiling liquid. Reduce heat and simmer gently for 2 hours or until meat is tender.
- Remove scum from liquid surface and add salt.
- Garnish and serve hot.

Chicken with Assorted Mushrooms

Preparation: 15 minutes   Cooking: 10 minutes

Ingredients

Button mushrooms	1/2 can (385 g), halved
Straw mushrooms	1/2 can (425 g), halved
Oyster or abalone mushrooms	1/2 can (425 g), halved
Dried Chinese mushrooms	7, soaked to soften, stems discarded and halved
Chicken	240 g, cut into strips
Cooking oil	3 Tbsp
Garlic	3 cloves, peeled and minced

Seasoning

Light soy sauce	2 tsp
Salt	1 tsp
Sugar	1 tsp
Ground white pepper	1/4 tsp
Sesame oil	1 tsp
Cornflour (cornstarch)	2 tsp

Sauce (combined)

Chicken stock	250 ml
Oyster sauce	1 Tbsp
Light soy sauce	2 tsp
Sugar	1 tsp
Sesame oil	1/2 tsp
Salt	1/4 tsp
Ground white pepper	1/4 tsp
Cornflour (cornstarch)	1 Tbsp

Ingredients to be chopped

Spring onion (scallion)	1
Coriander leaves (cilantro)	1 sprig
Red chilli	1

Method

- Separately soak button, straw, oyster or abalone and Chinese mushrooms in water for at least 15 minutes. Drain before use.
- Into a mixing bowl, put chicken and seasoning ingredients. Mix well and set aside.
- Heat 1 Tbsp oil in a wok until hot. Stir-fry Chinese mushrooms until fragrant, then remove and set aside.
- Add 1 Tbsp oil to heated wok and lightly brown garlic. Add chicken strips and fry for 2 minutes. Remove and set aside.
- Heat remaining 1 Tbsp oil in wok, add button mushrooms, then straw and oyster mushrooms and stir-fry for 2 minutes. Return Chinese mushrooms and chicken to wok and mix well.
- Pour in combined sauce ingredients and bring to the boil. When liquid thickens, add chopped ingredients.
- Dish out and serve hot.

Paper-wrapped Chicken

Preparation: 10 minutes Cooking: 15 minutes Makes 14 packages

Ingredients

Chicken	1, about 1.5 kg, cut into 14 pieces
Greaseproof paper bags	14, each 15 x 10 cm
Corn oil	1 Tbsp
Sesame oil	1 tsp
Cooking oil for deep-frying	

Seasoning

Coriander leaves (cilantro)	2 sprigs, chopped
Spring onions (scallions)	2, chopped
Garlic	1 bulb, peeled and ground
Ginger juice	extracted from 5-cm knob, peeled
Rice wine	1/2 Tbsp
Five-spice powder	1 tsp
Oyster sauce	3 Tbsp
Light soy sauce	2 Tbsp
Sesame oil	1 tsp
Dark soy sauce	1 tsp
Salt	1 tsp
Sugar	1/2 tsp
Ground white pepper	1/2 tsp
Tapioca flour	2 rounded (heaped) Tbsp

Garnishing

Cucumber slices
Tomato slices

Method

- Put chicken into a large bowl. Add all seasoning ingredients and mix thoroughly. Leave for at least 3 hours.
- Meanwhile, combine corn and sesame oil. Then, lightly grease the interior of each greaseproof paper bag with oil mixture.
- Fill greased bags with chicken, then fold and staple opening to secure.
- Heat oil for deep-frying in a wok until hot. Lower in packages and fry until chicken is cooked, takes about 15 minutes.
- Drain fried packages in a colander, then garnish and serve hot.

Note: Ready-made greaseproof paper bags for paper-wrapped chicken are available in Chinese sundry shops and supermarkets.

Dry Chicken Curry

Preparation: 15 minutes Cooking: 25 minutes

Ingredients

Chicken	1, about 1 kg
Salt	2 tsp
Cooking oil	100 ml
Pure coconut cream (*pati santan*)	250 ml, squeezed from 1 grated coconut
Lemon juice	squeezed from 1 lemon, or juice of 1 lime (*limau nipis*)

Ingredients to be ground

Red chillies	10
Dried chillies	10, soaked
Shallots	15, peeled
Garlic	8 cloves, peeled
Turmeric (*kunyit*)	2.5-cm knob, peeled

Method

- Cut chicken into bite-size pieces, then season with ground ingredients and salt. Set aside for 3 hours.
- Heat oil in a wok and fry seasoned chicken until lightly browned.
- Add coconut cream and simmer over low heat, stirring occasionally, until chicken is tender and gravy dry.
- Just before dishing out, add lemon juice.

Chinese Mustard with Crabmeat

Preparation: 20 minutes Cooking: 10 minutes

Ingredients

Chinese mustard (*gai choy*)	1 kg, separated into individual leaves
Bicarbonate of (baking) soda	1 tsp
Cooking oil	2 Tbsp
Garlic	5 cloves, peeled and minced
Button mushrooms	6, large, sliced
Crabs	600 g, steamed until cooked and meat extracted
Egg	1, lightly beaten

Sauce (combined)

Fresh chicken stock	500 ml
Salt	1 tsp
Sugar	1/2 tsp
Sesame oil	1/2 tsp
Ground white pepper	1/4 tsp
Cornflour (cornstarch)	1 Tbsp

Method

- Trim off and discard leafy parts of Chinese mustard, then cut into 7.5-cm lengths.
- Half fill a wok with water and bring to the boil, then stir in bicarbonate of soda and 1 tsp oil.
- Add Chinese mustard and boil for 3–4 minutes. Remove and immerse in a basin of cold water. Rinse and drain.
- Heat 5 tsp oil in a wok and lightly brown garlic. Add mushroom slices, then Chinese mustard lengths and stir-fry briskly for 1 minute.
- Pour in combined sauce ingredients and bring to the boil. Add crabmeat.
- When liquid thickens, gradually stir in egg. Dish out and serve immediately.

Chicken Wing Drumsticks

Preparation: 30 minutes Cooking: 12 minutes Makes 24

Ingredients

Chicken wings	12
Cooking oil for deep-frying	

Seasoning

Ginger juice	1 Tbsp
Rice wine	1 tsp
Sugar	1 tsp
Salt	1 tsp
Five-spice powder	1/4 tsp

Batter (combined)

Rice flour	3 Tbsp
Plain (all-purpose) flour	3 Tbsp
Baking powder	1 tsp
Salt	1/4 tsp
Five-spice powder	a pinch
Water	8 Tbsp, or enough for batter to reach a runny consistency

Chilli Sauce (combined and boiled)

Red chillies	12
Garlic	3 cloves, peeled
Ginger	2.5-cm knob, peeled
Oyster sauce	2 Tbsp
Tomato sauce (ketchup)	1 Tbsp
Vinegar	1/2 Tbsp
Sugar	1 tsp
Cooking oil	1 Tbsp

Garnishing

Cucumber slices
Tomato slices
Pineapple slices

Method

- Cut off tips of chicken wings, then cut each wing into two at the joint.
- With each wing segment, push meat to one end of bone with fingers and turn skin inside out to form a drumstick.
- Into a mixing bowl, put drumsticks and seasoning ingredients. Mix well and leave for 1 hour.
- Heat oil for deep-frying in a wok. Dip drumsticks into combined batter ingredients before frying until light golden brown.
- Serve hot with chilli sauce as a dip and, if desired, garnished.

Fried Yam Rings with Mixed Vegetables

Preparation: 10 minutes Steaming: 25–30 minutes Cooking: 8 minutes

Ingredients

Yam (taro)	1 kg, peeled and cut into cubes, clean weight of about 760 g should result
Salt	$1\frac{1}{2}$ tsp
Five-spice powder	1 tsp
Sugar	2 dsp
Cooking oil	as needed
Wheat starch flour (*tang meen fun*)	60 g
Chinese lettuce	1 small bunch, for garnishing
Filling*	1 recipe (page 123)

Method

- Prepare a steamer for use. When water is boiling rapidly, put in yam cubes and steam for 25–30 minutes or until soft.
- Mash yam cubes while still hot until lump-free. Mix in salt, five-spice powder, sugar and oil.
- When well combined, add wheat starch flour and knead well. Halve resulting yam dough.
- Lightly flour board and hands with wheat starch flour. Shape each dough portion into a hollow ring, 15 cm in diameter.
- Place each yam ring on a flat colander for deep-frying.
- Heat sufficient oil for deep-frying in a wok until hot. Reduce heat to medium and deep-fry yam rings, one at a time, for about 4 minutes or until golden.
- Place drained yam rings on a serving dish garnished with lettuce.
- Prepare filling. When done, fill yam rings with diced chicken with cashew nuts and serve immediately.

Note: Choose a good powdery yam for this recipe.

Fried Yam Bean and Cloud Ear Fungus

Preparation: 15 minutes Cooking: 10 minutes

Ingredients

Chicken or pork	240 g, cut into strips
Cooking oil	3 Tbsp
Garlic	3 cloves, peeled
Yam bean (*bangkuang*)	240 g, peeled and cut into strips
Dried cloud ear fungus (*wun yee*)	4 pieces, soaked and cut into thin strips
Cornflour (cornstarch)	1 Tbsp, mixed with 1 Tbsp water to make thickener

Seasoning

Light soy sauce	2 tsp
Sesame oil	1/2 tsp
Salt	1/2 tsp
Ground white pepper	1/2 tsp
Sugar	1/2 tsp
Cornflour (cornstarch)	2 tsp

Sauce (combined)

Fresh chicken stock	250 ml
Dark soy sauce	1 tsp
Sesame oil	1 tsp
Light soy sauce	2 tsp
Sugar	1 tsp
Salt	1 tsp
Ground white pepper	1/4 tsp

Garnishing

Spring onion (scallion)	1, cut into 5-cm lengths
Coriander leaves (cilantro)	2 sprigs, cut into 5-cm lengths

Method

- Mix chicken or pork strips and seasoning ingredients together. Leave for 30 minutes.
- Heat 1 Tbsp oil in a wok and brown garlic. Add meat and fry over high heat for 1 minute. Dish out. Set aside.
- Heat 2 Tbsp oil in a clean wok until hot. Add yam bean, stir-fry and cover wok for 1 minute. Uncover, add fungus and stir-fry quickly. Add sauce ingredients and bring to the boil.
- Return fried meat to wok, then stir in thickener. Garnish and serve hot.

Fried Lemon Chicken

Preparation: 10 minutes Cooking: 15 minutes

Ingredients

Chicken	1, about 1.5 kg, cut into 2.5-cm pieces
Light soy sauce	2 dsp
Sesame oil	2 tsp
Ground white pepper	1/2 tsp
Salt	3 tsp
Cornflour (cornstarch)	4 Tbsp
Cooking oil	as needed
Plum sauce	3 Tbsp, mixed with 2 Tbsp water
Sugar	4 dsp, mixed with 3 Tbsp lemon or lime (*limau nipis*) juice
Coriander leaves (cilantro)	3 sprigs

Method

- Season chicken pieces with soy sauce, sesame oil, pepper and salt. Leave for 30 minutes. Just before frying chicken, mix in cornflour.
- Heat sufficient oil for deep-frying in a wok until hot. Reduce heat before lowering in seasoned chicken.
- Fry chicken pieces, stirring frequently, for 10 minutes or until golden brown. Remove with a perforated ladle and drain.
- Heat 1 Tbsp oil in a clean wok. Add fried chicken and diluted plum sauce. Stir-fry for 1 minute, then add combined sugar and lemon or lime juice and stir-fry briskly.
- Serve hot, garnished with coriander.

Kuih Bingka Special

Preparation: 20 minutes Baking: 1 hour 20 minutes

Ingredients

Eggs	2, lightly beaten
Young tapioca	4 cups, grated
Sugar	450 g
Skinned coconut	1/2, about 240 g, finely grated
Coconut milk	315 ml, squeezed 1/2 grated coconut with sufficient water added
Plain (all-purpose) flour	60 g
Butter	60 g, at room temperature
Evaporated milk	4 Tbsp
Salt	1/4 tsp

Method

- Reserve and set aside a little of the beaten eggs for glazing later.
- Into a large bowl, put all remaining ingredients and mix thoroughly. When well combined, pour into an ungreased 21.5-cm square cake tin.
- Bake in an oven preheated to 205°C/400°F for 1 hour 20 minutes.
- Brush surface with reserved egg and bake for 3 minutes more or until top is firm and light golden.
- Remove from oven and leave to cool thoroughly before cutting into 2-cm thick slices.

Note: If you have a blender (food processor), cut tapioca into very small pieces, discarding the central fibre, and blend until fine.

Fried Bean Curd with Chilli

Preparation: 15 minutes Cooking: 8 minutes

Ingredients

Soft bean curd (*tau fu*)	2 pieces
Chicken or pork	90 g, minced
Cooking oil	2 Tbsp
Garlic	4 cloves, peeled and minced
Red chillies	3, seeded and minced
Preserved soy beans (*tau cheo*)	2 tsp, minced
Leek	1 stalk, diagonally sliced
Spring onions (scallions)	2, chopped

Seasoning

Light soy sauce	1/2 tsp
Salt	1/2 tsp
Sesame oil	1/4 tsp
Ground white pepper	a pinch

Sauce (combined)

Fresh chicken stock or water	125 ml
Oyster sauce	1 tsp
Sugar	1/2 tsp
Sesame oil	1/2 tsp
Salt	1/2 tsp
Dark soy sauce	1/2 tsp
Ground white pepper	1/4 tsp
Cornflour (cornstarch)	2 tsp

Method

- Cut each bean curd piece into 4-cm pieces.
- Into a mixing bowl, put meat and seasoning ingredients. Mix well and leave for 15 minutes.
- Heat oil in a wok. Fry garlic and chillies until fragrant.
- Add preserved soy beans and fry until aromatic. Then, add minced meat followed by leek and stir for 30 seconds more.
- Add bean curd and stir-fry for 2 minutes, breaking them gently with frying spatula.
- Pour in combined sauce ingredients and bring to the boil.
- When liquid thickens, add spring onions and dish out. Serve hot with rice.

Jemput Pisang

Preparation: 10 minutes   Cooking: 10 minutes   Makes approximately 40

Ingredients

Eggs	2
Sugar	30 g
Salt	1/4 tsp
Coconut milk	125 ml, squeezed from 1/2 grated coconut with sufficient water added
Bananas (*rastali* variety)	5, medium, mashed
Cooking oil for deep-frying	

Ingredients to be sifted together

Self-raising flour	120 g
Cornflour (cornstarch)	30 g
Baking powder	1 tsp

Method

- Whisk eggs and sugar until light and fluffy.
- Add salt and fold in sifted ingredients alternately with coconut milk.
- Add mashed bananas and mix well.
- Heat oil in a wok and fry tablespoonfuls of batter until golden brown.
- Drain well before serving.

Fried Hokkien Mee, KL Style

Preparation: 20 minutes   Cooking: 12 minutes

Ingredients

Prawns (shrimps)	150 g, small, peeled
Squid	5, small, cut into rings
Sesame oil	1/2 tsp
Ground white pepper	1/4 tsp
Light soy sauce	1/2 Tbsp
Cooking oil	2 Tbsp
Shallots	3, peeled and sliced
Chicken or pork fat	120 g, diced
Garlic	4 cloves, peeled and minced
Fish cake	6 slices
Chinese flowering cabbage (*chye sim*)	3–4 stalks, cut into 5-cm lengths
Fresh yellow (Hokkien) noodles	450 g
Water	500 ml
Thick dark soy sauce	1 Tbsp
Lettuce leaves	a few, cut into strips
*Sambal Belacan**	1 recipe

Method

- Into a mixing bowl, put prawns, squids, sesame oil, pepper and light soy sauce. Mix well and set aside.
- Heat oil in a wok and fry shallots until brown and crisp. Remove and set aside.
- Reheat wok and add chicken or pork fat. Fry until crisp. Remove fat crisps with a perforated ladle, leaving oil behind.
- When wok is smoking hot, add garlic, prawns and squids and fish cake. Then, add Chinese flowering cabbage and stir-fry for a few seconds before adding noodles. Fry for 2 minutes.
- Add water and thick dark soy sauce. Stir to combine sauce and cover wok for 1 minute.
- Uncover and add crisp-fried shallot slices and fat crisps.
- Serve hot, sprinkled with lettuce strips and accompanied with a small dish of sambal belacan.

*Sambal Belacan

Dried prawn (shrimp) paste (*belacan*)	5 x 5 x 0.5-cm piece
Red chillies	8
Kalamansi limes (*limau kesturi*)	3

Method

- Roast dried prawn paste in a clean pan over low heat until fragrant.
- While hot, pound roasted paste with red chillies until smooth. Transfer to a small dish and squeeze on lime juice.

Tau Fu Fah

Preparation: 25 minutes   Cooking: 25 minutes   Makes 12 servings

Ingredients

Soy beans	300 g
Water	3 litres
Cornflour (cornstarch)	45 g
Natural calcium sulfate (gypsum or *sekko fun*)	1 tsp, sifted
Hot water	125 ml
Syrup*	1 recipe

Method

- Wash and soak soy beans for at least 5 hours or preferably overnight. Drain before use.
- Blend ready-soaked soy beans in an electric blender (food processor), half at a time, with 375 ml water, until fine.
- Strain blended mixture using a piece of fine muslin cloth and squeeze pulp until dry. Add a little more water and squeeze again. Reserve soy bean pulp to make soy bean milk.
- Using a clean piece of fine muslin cloth, strain concentrated soy bean milk once more, this time into a large cooking pot.
- Add remaining water. Bring to the boil over moderate heat, stirring all the time with a wooden spoon, takes 15–20 minutes. Remove bubbles from the surface while stirring.
- Before soy bean milk reaches the boil, blend cornflour and calcium sulfate with 125 ml hot water until dissolved. Pour into a fairly large aluminium pot — a medium rice cooker pot will do nicely.
- As soon as soy bean milk reaches the boil, pour immediately, from a height of about 30 cm, over cornflour mixture. Quickly remove surface bubbles with a ladle and cover pot with a towel. Place lid over the towel and leave undisturbed for at least 40 minutes to set before serving.
- To serve, carefully scoop thin layers of bean curd into individual small bowls. Add 1½–2 Tbsp syrup to each bowl and serve either hot or cold.

*Syrup

Sugar	420 g
Water	315 ml
Ginger	2.5-cm knob, peeled
Screwpine (*pandan*) leaves	3, washed and knotted

Method

- Into a small saucepan, put all ingredients and bring to the boil, stirring until sugar dissolves.
- Remove from heat and strain.

Soy Bean Milk

Soy bean pulp	as reserved
Water	1.5 litres
Sugar	200 g
Screwpine (*pandan*) leaves	4, washed and knotted

Method

- Into a large pot, put all ingredients and bring to the boil, stirring frequently.
- Allow to simmer for 5 minutes, then strain using a piece of muslin cloth. When cool, refrigerate and serve as a drink.

Kuih Lapis

Preparation: 20 minutes Cooking: 50 minutes

Ingredients

Tapioca flour	105 g
Green (mung) bean flour	30 g
Wet rice flour	700 g
Coconut milk	1.375 litres, squeezed from $1^{1}/_{2}$ grated coconuts with sufficient water added
Syrup*	1 recipe
Red food colouring	a few drops

Method

- Sift tapioca and green bean flours together into a bowl. Add rice flour, then gradually pour in coconut milk and mix to a smooth batter.
- Gradually add syrup to flour mixture, stirring all the time until it is well blended.
- Divide flour mixture into 2 portions. Add a few drops of red food colouring to one portion and blend well. Leave the other uncoloured.
- Prepare a steamer for use. When water is boiling rapidly, place a deep, 25–27-cm round pan into steamer.
- Pour 1 cup white batter into pan, then secure cover on steamer and steam over moderate heat for 4 minutes.
- Remove cover and wipe underside with a dry towel, then pour 1 cup pink batter over cooked white layer. Steam for 4 minutes.
- Repeat white, then pink layers, alternating until both batters are used up. The last layer should be pink.
- For the final layer, add 1–2 drops red food colouring to pink batter for a stronger, richer colour.
- When done, remove cake and leave to cool thoroughly, takes at least 6–7 hours, before cutting.

*Syrup

Sugar	600 g
Water	250 ml
Screwpine (*pandan*) leaves	3, washed and knotted

Method

- Combine all ingredients in a pot and bring to the boil, stirring to dissolve sugar completely.
- When done, strain and leave to cool.

Note: Use a plastic knife or spatula to cut kuih lapis. The spatula supplied with an electric mixer will do beautifully.

Diced Chicken with Cashew Nuts

Preparation: 20 minutes Cooking: 10 minutes

Ingredients

Chicken breast meat	1 whole, cut into 1.25-cm cubes
Corn oil	3 Tbsp
Dried Chinese mushrooms	6, soaked to soften, stems discarded and diced
Onion	1, peeled and diced
Young corn	1 can (425 g), diced
Green capsicums (bell peppers)	2, diced
Carrot	1, medium, peeled if desired, diced and parboiled
Cashew nuts	90 g, roasted
Coriander leaves (cilantro)	2 sprigs, for garnishing

Seasoning

Sugar	1 tsp
Sesame oil	1 tsp
Salt	1 tsp
Rice wine	1 tsp
Cornflour (cornstarch)	1 tsp
Corn oil	1/2 Tbsp

Sauce (combined)

Fresh chicken stock	250 ml
Oyster sauce	2 dsp
Light soy sauce	1 tsp
Sesame oil	1 tsp
Rice wine	1 tsp
Sugar	1/2 tsp
Salt	1/2 tsp
Cornflour (cornstarch)	1 Tbsp

Method

- Into a mixing bowl, put chicken cubes and seasoning ingredients. Mix well and leave for at least 30 minutes.
- Heat 1 Tbsp oil in a wok. Stir-fry mushrooms for 1 minute and dish out.
- To heated wok, add seasoned chicken and stir-fry until cooked. Remove and wash wok.
- Heat 2 Tbsp oil in a clean wok. Fry onion pieces until transparent and fragrant.
- Return fried chicken and mushrooms to wok, then add young corn and stir-fry for 1–2 minutes.
- Add green capsicums, carrot and cashew nuts. Stir in sauce ingredients.
- Dish out and serve hot, garnished with coriander.

Serimuka Keledek

Preparation: 20 minutes Cooking: 1 hour

Ingredients

Yellow-fleshed sweet potatoes	700 g, steamed, peeled and mashed
Tapioca flour	180 g, sifted
Coconut cream	440 ml, squeezed from 1 grated coconut with a little water added, reserved for topping
Coconut milk	250 ml, squeezed from same grated coconut with sufficient water added.
Salt	3 tsp
Yellow food colouring	3–4 drops
Topping*	1 recipe

Method

- Into a mixing bowl, put mashed sweet potatoes, tapioca flour, coconut milk, salt and yellow food colouring. Mix well.
- Transfer mixture to a 25–27-cm round pan and steam for 20 minutes or until cooked.
- Remove pan from steamer. Pour prepared topping over cooked sweet potato layer, then return to steamer.
- Steam over medium heat for 25 minutes more. When done, leave to cool thoroughly before cutting.

*Topping

Eggs	3, large
Sugar	180 g
Coconut cream	as reserved
Tapioca flour	45 g, sifted
Salt	1/4 tsp
Screwpine (*pandan*) juice	1 Tbsp, obtained by blending (processing) or pounding 6–7 screwpine leaves with a little water
Green food colouring	2–3 drops

Method

- Put eggs and sugar into a bowl. Stir to combine; do not beat.
- Mix in coconut cream, tapioca flour and salt. Lastly, stir in screwpine juice and green food colouring.
- Strain to remove lumps.

Pahang

Pahang is the largest state in Peninsular Malaysia and within its borders are the famous hill resorts of Cameron Highlands, Fraser's Hill and Genting Highlands. Like Kelantan and Terengganu, there are stretches of fine beaches dotted with picturesque fishing villages, unhurried and leisurely. Kuantan, its bustling capital, has rapidly developed into a popular holiday resort with modern amenities.

Malaysia's longest river, the Sungei Pahang, and its tributaries are teeming with freshwater fish like *ikan jelawat*, *ikan kelah*, and *ikan kerai*. They are in high demand and are highly priced. Thick tropical jungle covers large tracts of Pahang. Predominantly rural, like the states of Kelantan and Terengganu, typical east coast cottage industries like silverware crafting, silk weaving and batik printing flourish here.

Malay food with the east coast flavour is relatively simple to prepare and the locals use mild spices enlivened with chillies and fragrant roots.

Gulai Botok

Preparation: 20 minutes   Cooking: 30 minutes

Ingredients

Spanish mackerel (*ikan tenggiri*)	2 slices, each 9-cm thick
Salt	as needed
Dried sour fruit (*asam gelugur*)	6 pieces
Coconut milk	750 ml, squeezed from 1 grated coconut with sufficient water added
Pea aubergines (*terung pipit/rembang*)	60 g
Terung asam	3, or 3 pieces dried sour fruit

Ingredients to be finely ground

Bird's eye chillies (*cili padi*)	30
Turmeric (*kunyit*)	2.5-cm knob, peeled

Method

- Rub fish with 2 tsp salt and dried sour fruit slices, then refrigerate overnight.
- On cooking day, lower fish into a saucepan of boiling water and simmer until fish is cooked. Flake cooked fish and lightly mash with a spoon.
- Into a pot, put mashed fish, ground ingredients, coconut milk, pea aubergines and *terung asam*. Cook over low heat, stirring frequently, for 15–20 minutes or until oil separates. Add salt to taste.

Note: Terung pipit grows wild. It is green in colour and the size of green peas with lots of tiny seeds. When cooked, it tastes like aubergines (eggplants/ brinjals). It is known as *terung rembang* in some other states, such as Negeri Sembilan and Perak. *Terung asam* is yellow in colour and very sour. If unavailable, use dried sour fruit (*asam gelugur*) as a substitute.

Gulai Ikan

Preparation: 15 minutes Cooking: 15 minutes

Ingredients

Spanish mackerel (*ikan tenggiri*)	2 thick slices
Salt	as needed
Ground white pepper	1 tsp
Coconut cream	250 ml, squeezed from 1 grated coconut with a little water added
Coconut milk	250 ml, squeezed from the same grated coconut with sufficient water added
Dried sour fruit (*asam gelugur*)	2 pieces

Ingredients to be ground

Bird's eye chillies (*cili padi*)	10
Turmeric (*kunyit*)	2.5-cm knob, peeled
Galangal (*lengkuas*)	2 slices, peeled
Lemon grass (*serai*)	1 stalk, sliced

Method

- Season fish with 1 tsp salt and pepper.
- Into a pot, put ground ingredients and mix in coconut milk. Add dried sour fruit slices. Bring to a slow boil.
- Add fish and coconut cream. Stir carefully until gravy thickens and fish is tender. Add salt to taste.

Masak Tempoyak Ikan Jelawat

Preparation: 15 minutes Cooking: 15 minutes

Ingredients

Sultan fish (*ikan jelawat*)	1, or Malaysian mahseer (*ikan kelah*) or Lemon-fin barb (*ikan kerai*)
Salt	as needed
Dried sour fruit (*asam gelugur*)	4 pieces
Water	1 litre

Ingredients to be ground

Fermented durian (*tempoyak*)	2 Tbsp (page 146)
Bird's eye chillies (*cili padi*)	10
Turmeric (*kunyit*)	6-mm piece, peeled
Polygonum leaves (*daun kesum*)	5 sprigs

Method

- Rub fish with 1 tsp salt and dried sour fruit slices, then set aside for 15 minutes.
- Wash fish and put into a pot together with ground ingredients and 1 tsp salt. Add water and bring to the boil.
- Reduce heat to low and simmer for 10 minutes more or until fish is cooked, taking care not to overcook fish.
- Serve hot with rice.

Note: *Ikan jelawat, ikan kelah* and *ikan kerai* are freshwater river fish. *Ikan kelah* is the most sought-after fish with soft scales and is usually cooked without removing the scales.

Rendang Daging

Preparation: 20 minutes Cooking: 1 hour 30 minutes

Ingredients

Beef	600 g, cut into 2.5-cm pieces
Black peppercorns	1 tsp, ground
Salt	as needed
Coconut milk	1.25 litres, squeezed from $1\frac{1}{2}$ grated coconuts with sufficient water added
Dried sour fruit (*asam gelugur*)	1 piece
Lemon grass (*serai*)	2 stalks, lightly crushed
Turmeric leaves (*daun kunyit*)	2

Ingredients to be ground

Dried chillies	15, soaked
Bird's eye chillies (*cili padi*)	15
Galangal (*lengkuas*)	2.5-cm knob, peeled
Turmeric (*kunyit*)	2.5-cm, knob, peeled
Ginger	2.5-cm knob, peeled
Shallots	15, peeled
Garlic	5 cloves, peeled

Method

- Season meat with ground black peppercorns and 1 tsp salt. Leave for 30 minutes.
- Into a pot, put ground ingredients and add coconut milk. Bring to a slow boil.
- Add seasoned meat, dried sour fruit slice, lemon grass and turmeric leaves. Simmer gently for 1 hour 15 minutes–1 hour 30 minutes or until meat is tender and gravy thick and oily.
- Add salt to taste. Discard lemon grass and turmeric leaves before serving.

Pincuk Daging

Preparation: 15 minutes Cooking: 1 hour

Ingredients

Beef	600 g
Pure coconut cream (*pati santan*)	squeezed from 1 grated coconut
Skinned coconut	$\frac{1}{2}$, grated, for *kerisik* (page 11)
Shallots	10, peeled and sliced
Black peppercorns	2 tsp, finely ground
Salt	1 tsp
Lime (*limau nipis*) juice	squeezed from 1 lime

Method

- Bring a saucepan of water to the boil. Add beef and leave to boil until tender. When done, drain and cut into 5-cm square slices.
- Into a mixing bowl, put beef slices and all remaining ingredients. Mix well.
- Serve with rice.

Note: Pincuk daging is usually served in *kenduris*, or social gatherings that involve the sharing of food and communal prayer sessions.

Masak Acar Tauco

Preparation: 15 minutes   Cooking: 12 minutes

Ingredients

Cucumbers	2, medium
Onions	2, peeled
Cooking oil	3 Tbsp
Shallots	5, peeled and sliced
Garlic	2 cloves, peeled and sliced
Ginger	1.25-cm knob, peeled and chopped
Dried anchovies (*ikan bilis*)	45 g, heads and entrails removed, chopped
Preserved soy beans (*tau cheo*)	2 Tbsp, coarsely ground
Tamarind pulp (*asam Jawa*)	1 Tbsp, mixed with 375 ml water and strained
Green chillies	10, split lengthways without cutting through
Salt (optional)	a pinch

Method

- Quarter each cucumber lengthways and discard seed portions, then slice into 4-cm strips. At the centre of each strip, make 2 slits without cutting through. Set aside.
- Slice off tapered tops of peeled onions. Then, make 2 cuts, forming an 'X', across newly exposed surfaces without cutting through. Prepared onions become flower-like with cooking (see photo, right).
- Heat oil in a wok. Lightly brown shallots, garlic, ginger and dried anchovies.
- Then, add preserved soy beans and fry until fragrant.
- Add tamarind juice and bring to a slow boil. Add onions and cucumbers, then green chillies. Simmer for a few minutes, taking care not to overcook cucumbers. If necessary, add a pinch of salt.

Note: Masak acar tauco is very often served in *kenduris*.

Ayam Golek, Pahang Style

Preparation: 15 minutes Cooking: 20 minutes Grilling: 50–60 minutes

Ingredients

Chicken	1, about 1.5 kg, halved and with a few slits made on back and thighs
Salt	as needed
Ground turmeric (*kunyit serbuk*)	1 tsp, or 2.5-cm knob turmeric, peeled and ground
Chicken curry powder	1½ Tbsp
Sugar	1 Tbsp
Dried sour fruit (*asam gelugur*)	2 small pieces
Coconut milk	500 ml, squeezed from 1 grated coconut with sufficient water added

Ingredients to be ground

Dried chillies	25, soaked
Shallots	300 g, peeled
Lemon grass (*serai*)	2 stalks
Ginger	1.25-cm knob, peeled

Method

- Rub chicken with 2 tsp salt and turmeric. Set aside for 15 minutes.
- Into a saucepan, put ground ingredients and all remaining ingredients. Bring to a slow boil, stirring over low heat for about 20 minutes or until gravy is thick.
- Grill chicken over glowing charcoal for 15–20 minutes on each side or until chicken is browned and cooked.
- Spoon gravy over chicken and grill for 5 minutes more or until fragrant and oily.
- Transfer to a dish and serve, if desired, garnished with lettuce, cucumber, tomatoes and chillies.

Note: Chubb or Indian mackerel (*ikan kembung*) or black pomfret (*ikan bawal hitam*) can be grilled this way. Use 1½ Tbsp fish instead of chicken curry powder.

Hati Pari

Preparation: 15 minutes Cooking: 40 minutes

Ingredients

Rice flour	300 g
Palm sugar (*gula Melaka*)	120 g, chopped
Sugar	120 g
Water	125 ml
Screwpine (*pandan*) leaves	2, washed and knotted
Coconut milk	1.25 litres, squeezed from 1 1/2 grated coconut with sufficient water added
Banana leaf	1
Topping (*Minyak Muda*)*	1 recipe

Method

- Sift rice flour into a mixing bowl. Set aside.
- Into a pot, put both sugars, water and screwpine leaves. Melt sugar over low heat, stirring frequently. Strain syrup.
- Stir syrup and coconut milk into rice flour and blend until smooth. Strain mixture into a clean pot and cook over low heat until a lump of cooked dough forms.
- Transfer dough to an 27 x 18-cm shallow tin and, using banana leaf, smoothen surface while still hot.
- Sprinkle on topping. Leave to cool thoroughly before cutting.

*Topping (*Minyak Muda*)

Pure coconut cream (*pati santan*)	250 ml, squeezed from 1 grated coconut
Salt	a pinch

Method

- In a wok, cook coconut cream with salt over low heat, stirring with a wooden spatula, for 30 minutes. Oil will separate from coconut residue. Continue stirring until residue turns a rich brown. Remove from heat and drain for browned crisps.

Gulai Maman

Preparation: 15 minutes Cooking: 20 minutes

Ingredients

Maman vegetables	2 bunches
Salt	as needed
Spanish mackerel (*ikan tenggiri*)	2 thick slices
Dried sour fruit (*asam gelugur*)	3 pieces
Coconut milk	1 litre, squeezed from 1 grated coconut with sufficient water added

Ingredients to be ground

Bird's eye chillies (*cili padi*)	12
Turmeric (*kunyit*)	1.25-cm knob, peeled

Method

- Wash and drain *maman* vegetables. Mix with 1 tsp salt and lightly squeeze out the juice, then rinse thoroughly with water.
- Into a pot, put half the vegetables. Top with fish slices, 1 1/2 tsp salt, ground ingredients and dried sour fruit slices.
- Distribute remaining vegetables on top, then carefully pour in coconut milk to cover ingredients.
- Cook over low heat without stirring until gravy is thick.

Note: Leaves of the *maman* vegetable are clover- shaped and the size of red spinach. It is usually grown in the *padi* fields of Pahang before a new crop of *padi* is planted.

Laksa Pahang

Preparation: 30 minutes Cooking: 40 minutes Serves: 8–10

Ingredients

Chubo mackerels (*ikan kembung*)	8, medium–large
Salt	as needed
Screwpine (*pandan*) leaves	2, washed and knotted
Cooking oil	150 ml
Grated skinned coconut	120 g, for *kerisik* (page 11), ground
Coconut milk	2 litres, squeezed from 1 grated coconut with sufficient water added
Dried sour fruit (*asam gelugur*)	2 pieces
Sugar	1 tsp
Thick round rice (*laksa*) noodles	1 packet (600 g), scalded and drained

Ingredients to be ground

Dried chillies	30, soaked
Shallots	15, peeled
Lemon grass (*serai*)	2 stalks
Galangal (*lengkuas*)	2.5-cm knob, peeled
Ginger	1.25-cm knob, peeled
Ground turmeric (*kunyit serbuk*)	1 tsp
Fish curry powder	$1\frac{1}{2}$ Tbsp

Garnishing

Cucumber	1, shredded
Long (snake) beans	6–8, chopped and left uncooked
Bean sprouts	300 g, tailed
Onions	2, peeled and shredded
Turmeric leaves (*daun kunyit*)	2, finely sliced
Basil leaves	1 small bunch, finely sliced

Side Dip (combined)

Red chillies	8–10, ground
Dried prawn (shrimp) paste (*belacan*)	5 x 1.25-cm piece, toasted and ground separately
Salt	to taste

Method

- Rub fish with 2 tsp salt then boil in some water with screwpine leaves added. Leave to boil until fish is cooked. Flake and grind or blend (process) cooked fish until fine.
- Heat oil in a wok. Add ground ingredients and *kerisik*. Fry until fragrant and oil separates.
- Add ground fish, coconut milk, dried sour fruit, 2 tsp salt and sugar. Bring to a slow boil, then reduce heat and simmer for 20 minutes, stirring frequently.
- To serve, put some noodles into individual serving bowls. Top with a little of each garnishing ingredient, then ladle hot gravy over. Serve with side dip.

Puding Raja

Preparation: 10 minutes   Cooking: 15 minutes

Ingredients

Cooking oil for deep-frying	
Bananas (*lemak manis* or *susu* variety)	2 combs, about 24 bananas, peeled
Jala Emas*	1 recipe
Glacé (candied) cherries	5, sliced
Sauce**	1 recipe

Method

- Heat oil in a wok and deep-fry bananas, a few at a time, over low heat for 5 minutes or until golden.
- Drain on absorbent paper and arrange on a serving dish.
- Top with prepared jala emas.
- Decorate with cherry slices and serve with chilled sauce.

*Jala Emas

Sugar	240 g
Water	250 ml
Screwpine (*pandan*) leaves	2, washed and knotted

Ingredients to be lightly beaten

Duck's egg yolks	6
Egg yolk	1
Rose essence (extract)	1/2 tsp

Method

- Into a saucepan, put sugar, water and screwpine leaves. Bring to a slow boil, stirring until sugar dissolves. Discard screwpine leaves.
- Put a ladleful of beaten yolks into a fine tea strainer and drizzle over boiling syrup, using a circular motion.
- When egg net is cooked, stir carefully with a small ladle to give it an even coating of syrup. Then, using a perforated ladle, remove to a serving dish.
- Lightly separate jala emas with a chopstick or fork for use.

**Sauce

Evaporated milk	1 can (410 g)
Condensed milk	2 dsp
Egg	1, lightly beaten
Water	125 ml
Rose or vanilla essence (extract)	1/4 tsp

Method

- In a saucepan, combine evaporated and condensed milk, lightly beaten egg, water and essence. Bring to a slow boil, stirring continuously.
- Remove from heat and strain into a serving jug. Refrigerate.

Note: Bananas should not be too ripe, otherwise they will not keep their shape after frying. *Pisang lemak manis* and *pisang susu* are slightly larger and firmer than *pisang emas*. Puding raja and ayam golek, Pahang style (page 134) are very popular traditional dishes for royal weddings and royal festive celebrations in Pahang.

Dadar

Preparation: 20 minutes Cooking: 50 minutes Makes 18 pancakes

Ingredients

Plain (all-purpose) flour	300 g
Egg yolks	2, lightly beaten
Salt	$^1/_2$ tsp
Coconut milk	875 ml, squeezed from 1 grated coconut with sufficient water added
Vanilla essence (extract)	$^1/_2$ tsp
Green food colouring	a few drops
Cooking oil	
Coconut Milk Sauce*	1 recipe
Durian Sauce**	1 recipe

Method

- Sift flour into a mixing bowl. Add egg yolks and salt, then gradually blend in coconut milk.
- Stir in vanilla essence and green food colouring. Strain to remove lumps.
- Grease, then heat a 15–18-cm pan. Pour on a ladleful or about 4 Tbsp batter so a thin layer forms. Cook over very low heat for 1–2 minutes.
- Remove pancake and repeat until batter is used up.
- Arrange pancakes in 2 neat stacks. To serve, cut wedges from stacks and top with coconut milk sauce or durian sauce.

*Coconut Milk Sauce

Coconut milk	500 ml, squeezed from 1 grated skinned coconut with sufficient water added
Sugar	150 g
Egg yolks	2, lightly beaten
Salt	$^1/_4$ tsp
Screwpine (*pandan*) leaves	3, washed and knotted

Method

- Put all ingredients into a saucepan.
- Over low heat, stir continuously with a flat wooden spoon for about 15 minutes or until sauce thickens.

**Durian Sauce

Durian pulp	from 1 medium durian, do not discard seeds if desired
Coconut milk	1.25 litres, squeezed from 1 grated coconut with sufficient water added
Brown sugar	120 g
Salt	a pinch
Screwpine (*pandan*) leaves	4, washed and knotted

Method

- In a pot, combine all ingredients and stir over moderate heat until sauce thickens.
- Durian seeds become edible with cooking. If keeping the seeds, allow sauce to simmer, stirring occasionally, until seeds are cooked.

Perak

Perak, meaning the "Silver state", has a multiracial population which ensures a wide range of cuisines. Truly outstanding specialties are the Malay curry dishes, especially the *rendangs*. Methods of preparation are also as exotic as the names. Rendang Tok with slices of young coconut is *lemak* and extremely rich; both Rendang Terlagi-lagi and Rendang Dinding are redolent in thick black sauce and irresistibly delicious; good and spicy Daging Masak Pesamah and Ayam Rendang Pedas are all-time favourites; and although *tempoyak* (fermented salted durian) has a slightly unusual smell to the uninitiated, it is nevertheless appetising.

Ipoh, the state capital, is a municipality full of bustle and local character. The specialty here is *sar hor fun* (flat rice noodles) which is unrivalled for smoothness and soft texture. Apparently, this is due to the hardness of the water in the Perak region, but it must be partly attributable to the quality of the rice flour used, and to the skill of the maker. Whatever the reason, it remains a well-guarded secret.

Equally famous and just as unique as the Ipoh limestone caves are the Ipoh bean sprouts. Fat, crisp and almost tailless, they are indeed 'king' of all bean sprouts. This, too, has been attributed to the underground water of the Ipoh region, especially the Buntong region.

Ikan Asam Rebus with Pineapple

Preparation: 10 minutes Cooking: 25 minutes

Ingredients

Spanish mackerel (*ikan tenggiri*)	450 g, sliced
Salt	as needed
Water	625 ml
Dried sour fruit (*asam gelugur*)	2 pieces
Pineapple	1/2, peeled and sliced
Sugar	1 tsp

Ingredients to be ground

Red chillies	8, seeded
Bird's eye chillies (*cili padi*)	8
Lemon grass (*serai*)	2 stalks
Turmeric (*kunyit*)	1.25-cm knob, peeled
Shallots	10, peeled

Method

- Wash fish slices and rub with 1 tsp salt. Set aside.
- Into a pot, put ground ingredients and water, then bring to a slow boil.
- Add dried sour fruit slices and leave to boil over low heat for 10 minutes.
- Add pineapple slices and simmer for 5 minutes more.
- Add fish slices and all remaining ingredients. Cook for 5 minutes.
- Serve hot with white rice.

Ikan Terubuk Masak Asam Tempoyak

Preparation: 10 minutes   Cooking: 15 minutes

Ingredients

Hilsa or shad (*ikan terubuk*) or red snapper (*ikan merah*)	2 slices
Salt	as needed
Fermented durian (*tempoyak*)	3 Tbsp
Water	500 ml
Turmeric (*kunyit*)	1.25-cm knob, peeled and finely ground
Lemon grass (*serai*)	1 stalk, lightly crushed
Turmeric leaf (*daun kunyit*)	1
Sugar	1 tsp
Soy bean sprouts	450 g, tailed

Ingredients to be coarsely ground

Red chillies	4–5
Onion	1, peeled
Dried anchovies (*ikan bilis*)	30 g

Method

- Wash fish slices and rub with 1 tsp salt. Set aside.
- Except fish slices and bean sprouts, put all other ingredients, including those coarsely ground, into a pot. Mix well and bring to a slow boil.
- Reduce heat and simmer for 10 minutes, then add fish and bean sprouts. Simmer until cooked. Discard turmeric leaf before serving.

Note: To ferment durian, scrape durian flesh from the seeds. Mix with salt and leave in an airtight jar in the refrigerator for at least 3 days before use. *Tempoyak* can be kept refrigerated for months. *Tempoyak* is also commonly served as a *sambal* taken with rice. To serve sambal tempoyak, pound 4–5 chillies coarsely with a pinch of salt. Mix with 2 Tbsp *tempoyak* or serve separately.

Pindang Udang

Preparation: 25 minutes   Cooking: 10 minutes

Ingredients

Prawns (shrimps)	600 g, medium
Salt	as needed
Cooking oil	2 Tbsp
Shallots	7, peeled and sliced
Lemon grass (*serai*)	8 stalks, very finely sliced
Red chillies	3, diagonally sliced
Turmeric (*kunyit*)	2.5-cm knob, peeled and ground
Blimbing (*belimbing*)	4–5, halved lengthways
Coconut milk	250 ml, squeezed from 1/2 grated coconut with sufficient water added

Method

- Peel prawns but leave tails intact. Devein prawns, then rub with 1 tsp salt. Set aside.
- Heat oil in a wok. Fry shallots, lemon grass, chillies and turmeric.
- Add prawns and stir-fry continuously, then add blimbing and coconut milk. Bring to a slow boil.
- Let simmer for 1–2 minutes before stirring in salt to taste.

Rendang Tok

Preparation: 20 minutes Cooking: 2 hours–2 hours 30 minutes

Ingredients

Beef	1.5 kg
Shallots	150 g, peeled and sliced
Garlic	120 g, peeled and sliced
Ginger	150 g, peeled and shredded
Skinned coconut	1/2, grated, for *kerisik* (page 11)
Young but firm skinned coconut	1/2, cut into thin 5-cm slices
Pure coconut cream (*pati santan*)	squeezed from 5 grated coconuts
Salt	3 tsp or to taste

Ingredients to be ground

Ground coriander (*ketumbar serbuk*)	2 rounded (heaped) Tbsp
Ground chilli	2 Tbsp
Cumin seeds (*jintan manis biji*)	1 tsp
Fennel seeds (*jintan putih biji*)	1 tsp
Black peppercorns	1/2 tsp
Cardamoms (*buah pelaga*)	10
Cloves (*bunga cengkih*)	10
Cinnamon (*kayu manis*)	5-cm stick
Ground turmeric (*kunyit serbuk*)	1 tsp

Method

- Cut cleaned beef into 5-cm cubes. Set aside.
- Prepare marinade. Except beef and salt, put all other ingredients, including those ground, into a large bowl. Mix well. Add beef pieces and leave to marinate for 2 hours.
- Transfer meat and marinade to a pot. Bring to a slow boil, then simmer over low heat, stirring frequently, for 2 hours–2 hours 30 minutes.
- When meat is tender and almost black in colour and gravy dry, add salt to taste. To prevent meat and gravy from sticking to pot, stir continuously when gravy is almost dry.

Note: Rendang tok is popularly served in *kenduris*, as well as during festive celebrations with *nasi himpit* or compressed rice cakes (page 159). It keeps well in the refrigerator for at least a week.

Rendang Dinding

Preparation: 20 minutes Cooking: 1 hour 15 minutes

Ingredients

Beef	1 kg
Cooking oil	as needed
Onions	1 kg, peeled and sliced
Garlic	3 cloves, peeled and sliced
Ginger	5-cm knob, peeled and shredded
Thick dark soy sauce	1 dsp
Tamarind pulp (*asam Jawa*)	2 Tbsp, mixed with 750 ml water and strained
Brown sugar	2 Tbsp
Salt	2 rounded (heaped) tsp

Ingredients to be ground

Dried chillies	45
Garlic	5 cloves, peeled

Method

- Cut meat across grain and into 0.6-cm thick slices. Score slices lightly.
- Heat 250 ml oil in a wok. Fry onions, garlic and ginger for 5–7 minutes. Drain, then coarsely grind fried ingredients. Set aside.
- Heat 3 Tbsp oil in a clean wok and fry ground ingredients until oil separates.
- Add meat, then coarsely ground fried ingredients and soy sauce. Continue frying for 15 minutes.
- Add tamarind juice, then all remaining ingredients. Stir frequently over low heat until gravy is thick and meat tender.
- Serve with white rice or roti jala (page 214).

Rendang Terlagi-lagi

Preparation: 20 minutes Cooking: 1 hour

Ingredients

Cooking oil	125 ml
Beef	600 g, cut into 4-cm long slices, each 0.6-cm thick
Thick dark soy sauce	1 Tbsp
Dried chillies	20, soaked and ground
Lemon grass (*serai*)	4 stalks, crushed
Pure coconut cream (*pati santan*)	squeezed from 1 1/2 grated coconuts
Tamarind pulp (*asam Jawa*)	1 Tbsp, mixed with 5 Tbsp water and strained
Skinned coconut	1/2, grated, for *kerisik* (page 11)
Sugar	1 tsp
Salt	1 1/2 tsp or to taste

Ingredients to be ground

Shallots	300 g, peeled
Garlic	4 cloves, peeled
Ginger	2.5-cm knob, peeled

Method

- Heat oil in a wok. Fry beef slices over moderate heat for 15 minutes.
- Drain meat slices from oil and lightly pound them while still hot.
- Season cooked meat with soy sauce and leave for 1 hour.
- Reheat wok and fry ground chillies for 2–3 minutes.
- Add ground ingredients and lemon grass. Fry until fragrant and oil separates.
- Add seasoned beef and mix well. Then, add coconut cream and tamarind juice.
- Bring to the boil.
- Reduce heat and simmer until almost dry. Then, add all remaining ingredients and stir continuously until gravy is very thick.

Note: When you have tasted this *rendang* you will ask for more, hence the name rendang terlagi-lagi. Try it, you'll not be disappointed.

Rendang Daging Perak

Preparation: 20 minutes   Cooking: 1 hour 45 minutes

Ingredients

Beef	1 kg, cut into 2.5-cm cubes
Salt	as needed
Cooking oil	125 ml
Galangal (*lengkuas*)	2.5-cm knob, peeled and crushed
Lemon grass (*serai*)	2 stalks, crushed
Dried chillies	20, soaked and ground
Coconut milk	1.25 litres, squeezed from 2 grated coconuts with sufficient water added
Turmeric leaves (*daun kunyit*)	3, 2 finely cut

Ingredients to be ground

Galangal (*lengkuas*)	2.5-cm knob, peeled
Ginger	2.5-cm knob, peeled
Turmeric (*kunyit*)	2.5-cm knob, peeled
Lemon grass (*serai*)	3 stalks
Shallots	600 g, peeled
Garlic	1 bulb, peeled

Method

- Season meat with 1 tsp salt and set aside for 15 minutes.
- Heat oil in a wok. Fry galangal and lemon grass, then add ground chillies to fry.
- Add ground ingredients and stir-fry constantly over low heat until fragrant and oil separates.
- Add meat and stir-fry until liquid evaporates, then add coconut milk and the whole turmeric leaf. Bring to a slow boil, stirring constantly.
- Reduce heat further and cook for about 1 hour 30 minutes, stirring frequently. Remove and discard turmeric leaf.
- When meat is tender and gravy thick and oily, add all remaining ingredients. Remove from heat.

Daging Masak Pesamah

Preparation: 20 minutes   Cooking: 1 hour 30 minutes

Ingredients

Beef	600 g
Meat curry powder	10 Tbsp
Skinned coconut	1/2, grated, for *kerisik* (page 11)
Tamarind pulp (*asam Jawa*)	1 Tbsp, mixed with 250 ml water and strained
Cooking oil	100 ml
Shallots	5, peeled and sliced
Coconut milk	1 litre, squeezed from 1 grated coconut with sufficient water added
Sugar	1 tsp
Salt	2 tsp

Spices

Cinnamon (*kayu manis*)	5-cm stick
Cardamoms (*buah pelaga*)	2
Cloves (*bunga cengkih*)	4
Star anise (*bunga lawang*)	2 sections

Ingredients to be ground

Shallots	10, peeled
Garlic	4 cloves, peeled
Ginger	2.5-cm knob, peeled

Method

- Cut beef across grain and into thin slices. Set aside.
- Mix curry powder and *kerisik* with tamarind juice into a paste. If necessary, add a little extra water. Set aside.
- Heat oil in a pot and fry shallots for 2 minutes, then spices until fragrant.
- Add ground ingredients and fry for a few minutes.
- Add prepared paste and fry over moderate heat until fragrant and oil separates. If ground ingredients are sticking to pot, add a little coconut milk.
- Put in beef and add 250 ml coconut milk. Stir-fry rapidly to mix ingredients.
- Pour in remaining coconut milk, then add sugar and salt.
- Simmer over low heat, stirring frequently, until gravy is thick and almost dry and meat tender.

Kurma Ayam

Preparation: 20 minutes Cooking: 50 minutes

Ingredients

Chicken	1, about 1.5 kg
Salt	as needed
Cooking oil	4 Tbsp
Shallots	5, peeled and sliced
Garlic	1 clove, peeled and sliced
Ginger	2.5-cm knob, peeled and cut into strips
Kurma curry powder	3 heaped Tbsp, mixed with water into paste
Star anise (*bunga lawang*)	2 sections
Cloves (*bunga cengkih*)	5
Cardamoms (*buah pelaga*)	2
Cinnamon (*kayu manis*)	2.5-cm stick
Nutmeg (*buah pala*)	$^1/_4$ piece
Coconut milk	1 litre, squeezed from 1 grated coconut with sufficient water added
Onions	3, peeled and prepared as on page 132
Chinese celery	3 sprigs, chopped
Red chillies	2, sliced
Crisp-fried shallots	2 Tbsp

Ingredients to be ground

Shallots	10, peeled
Garlic	3 cloves, peeled
Ginger	2.5-cm knob, peeled
Poppy seeds	4 Tbsp
Fennel seeds (*jintan manis biji*)	1 Tbsp
Cumin seeds (*jintan putih biji*)	1 tsp
White peppercorns	1 Tbsp
Grated skinned coconut	2 Tbsp

Method

- Cut chicken into bite-sized pieces and season with 1 tsp salt.
- Heat oil in an earthen pot. Fry shallots, garlic and ginger until fragrant. Add curry paste and fry for 1 minute. Add ground ingredients, star anise, cloves, cardamoms, cinnamon and nutmeg. Fry until oil separates.
- Add chicken and fry for 5 minutes, then add coconut milk and onions. Bring to the boil, stirring constantly. Reduce heat and simmer until chicken is tender. Add remaining ingredients just before removing from heat.

Ayam Panggang

Preparation: 20 minutes Cooking: 10 minutes
Grilling: 30 minutes

Ingredients

Chicken	1, about 1.5 kg, cut into 6 pieces
Ground turmeric (*kunyit serbuk*)	1 rounded (heaped) tsp
Salt	as needed
Coconut cream	375 ml, squeezed from 1 grated coconut with a little water added
Sugar	1 tsp
Cooking oil for deep-frying	
Lemon grass (*serai*)	1 stalk, bulbous end lightly crushed for basting

Ingredients to be ground

Dried chillies	20, soaked
Shallots	12, peeled
Garlic	5 cloves, peeled
Ginger	1.25-cm knob, peeled
Young galangal (*lengkuas*)	2.5-cm knob, peeled
Turmeric (*kunyit*)	2.5-cm knob, peeled

Method

- Rub chicken pieces with ground turmeric and 2 tsp salt. Leave for 15 minutes.
- Into a mixing bowl, put ground ingredients, coconut cream, sugar and 1 tsp salt. Mix well and set aside.
- Heat oil for deep-frying and cook chicken pieces for 10 minutes or until half-cooked. Remove and drain well.
- Using crushed lemon grass, baste chicken with coconut cream mixture and grill, preferably over glowing charcoal.
- Baste chicken with coconut cream mixture at least 3 times on each side and grill until chicken is cooked.

Ayam Rendang Pedas

Preparation: 20 minutes   Cooking 1 hour

Ingredients

Chicken	1, about 2 kg, cut into bite-size pieces
Coconut cream	1 litre, squeezed from 2 grated coconuts with a little water added
Skinned coconut	1/2, grated, for *kerisik* (page 11)
Turmeric leaves (*daun kunyit*)	3, finely sliced
Kaffir lime leaves (*daun limau purut*)	3, finely sliced
Salt	2 tsp or to taste

Ingredients to be ground

Dried chillies	40, soaked
Shallots	300 g, peeled
Garlic	4 cloves, peeled
Ginger	5-cm knob, peeled
Lemon grass (*serai*)	6 stalks
Galangal (*lengkuas*)	2.5-cm knob, peeled
Ground turmeric (*kunyit serbuk*)	1 tsp

Method

- Into a wok, put chicken and ground ingredients.
- Stir in coconut cream and bring to a slow boil.
- Reduce heat and simmer, stirring occasionally, until gravy is thick.
- Add *kerisik* and stir continuously until gravy is very thick and oily and meat tender.
- Lastly, add sliced leaves and salt to taste. Remove from heat.

Rendang Ayam Perak

Preparation: 20 minutes Cooking: 40 minutes

Ingredients

Chicken	1, about 1.5 kg
Salt	as needed
Cooking oil	3 Tbsp
Galangal (*lengkuas*)	2.5-cm knob, peeled and crushed
Lemon grass (*serai*)	3 stalks, crushed
Coconut milk	750 ml, squeezed from $1^1/_2$ grated coconuts with sufficient water added
Turmeric leaves (*daun kunyit*)	2, finely sliced

Ingredients to be ground (A)

Dried chillies	20, soaked
Red chillies	3, seeded

Ingredients to be ground (B)

Galangal (*lengkuas*)	2.5-cm knob, peeled
Ginger	2.5-cm knob, peeled
Shallots	20, peeled
Garlic	1 small pod, peeled
Turmeric (*kunyit*)	2.5-cm knob, peeled
Lemon grass (*serai*)	3 stalks

Method

- Cut chicken into bite-sized pieces and season with 2 tsp salt. Set aside for 15 minutes.
- Heat oil in a wok. Fry galangal and lemon grass until fragrant. Add and fry ground ingredients (A) for 3–5 minutes, then ground ingredients (B) until fragrant and oil separates. Stir constantly to prevent mixture sticking to wok.
- Pour in coconut milk and cook over low heat, stirring constantly, for 10 minutes. When gravy is thickened, add chicken. Allow to simmer, stirring frequently, until chicken is almost cooked.
- To prevent chicken from being overcooked, drain and remove chicken, leaving gravy to simmer until really thick.
- Return chicken to wok, then add turmeric leaves and salt. Remove from heat and serve with rice.

Note: This dish has very little gravy and chicken must not be overcooked or *rendang* will look messy with flesh and bones separated.

Ipoh Bean Sprouts with Salted Fish

Preparation: 10 minutes Cooking: 5 minutes

Ingredients

Cooking oil	as needed
Salted fish	45 g, preferably threadfin (*ikan kurau/senangin*), washed and finely sliced
Garlic	3 cloves, peeled and minced
Light soy sauce	$^1/_2$ Tbsp
Sesame oil	$^1/_2$ Tbsp
Ipoh bean sprouts	300 g, washed and drained

Garnishing

Red chilli	1, seeded and cut into strips
Spring onion (scallion)	1, split and cut into 5-cm lengths
Coriander leaves (ciliantro)	1 sprig

Method

- Heat sufficient oil in a wok until hot. Add salted fish slices and fry over low heat until crisp and light golden brown. Drain and set aside. Discard oil.
- Heat 2 Tbsp oil in the same wok and lightly brown garlic. Remove and place on a serving dish. Mix in light soy sauce and sesame oil.
- Bring a saucepan half filled with water to a rapid boil. Lower in bean sprouts and scald for a few seconds. Drain well.
- To serving dish with prepared seasoning, add scalded bean sprouts. Mix to combine ingredients, then sprinkle on salted fish.
- Garnish and serve hot.

Note: Ipoh bean sprouts are especially crisp, fat and almost tailless. This has been attributed to the hardness of the underground water in the Ipoh district.

Pecal (Vegetable Salad)

Preparation: 30 minutes Cooking: 20 minutes

Ingredients

Firm bean curd (*tau kwa*)	2, diced and fried
Hard-boiled eggs	4, shelled and quartered
Cooking oil	as needed
Tamarind pulp (*asam Jawa*)	2 Tbsp
Water	as needed
Brown sugar	4 Tbsp
Black prawn (shrimp) paste (*hae ko*)	2 Tbsp, mixed with 1 Tbsp water
Salt	1/2 tsp or to taste
Roasted peanuts	300 g, coarsely ground

Vegetables

Water convolvulus (*kangkung*)	300 g, young shoots only, cut into 5-cm lengths
Young tapioca leaves	300 g, tender shoots only, cut into 5-cm lengths
Bean sprouts	150 g, tailed
Yam bean (*bangkuang*)	150 g, peeled and coarsely shredded
Long (snake) beans	150 g, cut into 5-cm lengths
Carrot	1, medium, peeled if desired and coarsely shredded
Cucumber	1, cored and coarsely shredded

Ingredients to be ground

Dried chillies	15, soaked
Dried prawn (shrimp) paste (*belacan*)	2.5-cm square piece, toasted

Garnishing

Shallots	10, peeled, sliced and crisp-fried
Garlic	3 cloves, peeled, sliced and crisp-fried

Method

- Except cucumber, separately scald all vegetables in boiling water. Do not overcook. Drain well and arrange on a dish together with cucumber, fried bean curd and hard-boiled eggs.
- Heat sufficient oil and fry tamarind pulp for 1 minute over low heat. Dish out, add 125 ml water and mix well, then strain for tamarind juice.
- Heat 1 Tbsp oil and fry ground ingredients over low heat until fragrant.
- Add tamarind juice and 315 ml water. Bring to the boil.
- Stir in brown sugar, diluted prawn paste and salt to taste. Remove from heat and stir in ground peanuts.
- Garnish vegetables, then serve with sauce on the side or pour sauce over vegetables and mix well just before serving.

Kerabu Tauge

Preparation: 20 minutes   Cooking: 10 minutes

Ingredients

Bean sprouts (*tauge*)	600 g, tailed
Dried prawns (shrimps) (*hae be*)	1 Tbsp, roasted and coarsely ground
Grated skinned coconut	2 Tbsp, for *kerisik* (page 11)
Shallots	6, peeled and sliced
Bird's eye chillies (*cili padi*)	20, sliced
Lime (*limau nipis*) juice	squeezed from 1 lime
Pure coconut cream (*pati santan*)	squeezed from 1/2 grated coconut
Salt	1/2 tsp

Method

- Scald bean sprouts in boiling water and drain well.
- Into a bowl, put bean sprouts and all remaining ingredients. Mix well.
- Serve with white rice.

Pajri Nanas

Preparation: 15 minutes Cooking: 15 minutes

Ingredients

Pineapple (*nanas*)	1, medium, peeled
Cooking oil	2 Tbsp
Shallots	6, peeled and sliced
Garlic	2 cloves, peeled and sliced
Ginger	1.25-cm knob, peeled and shredded
Meat curry powder	3 Tbsp, mixed with 4 Tbsp water into a paste
Dried prawns (shrimps) (*hae be*)	2 rounded (heaped) Tbsp, ground
Grated skinned coconut	5 Tbsp, for *kerisik* (page 11), ground
Coconut milk	500 ml, squeezed from 1/2 grated coconut with sufficient water added
Tamarind pulp (*asam Jawa*)	1 dsp, mixed with 2 Tbsp water and strained
Salt	1 tsp
Sugar	1 tsp

Spices

Cinnamon (*kayu manis*)	2.5-cm stick
Cloves (*bunga cengkih*)	6
Cardamoms (*buah pelaga*)	2
Star anise (*bunga lawang*)	1 section

Method

- Halve pineapple and cut into slices. Set aside.
- Heat oil in a wok. Lightly brown shallots, garlic and ginger, then add spices and fry until fragrant.
- Add curry paste and fry for 1 minute, then add dried prawns and *kerisik*. Fry until fragrant.
- Add pineapple slices, then coconut milk and bring to a slow boil.
- Add all remaining ingredients, simmer for 5 minutes and remove from heat.

Kerabu Nanas

Preparation: 15 minutes Cooking: 5 minutes

Ingredients

Pineapple (*nanas*)	1, small, peeled
Dried prawns (shrimps) (*hae be*)	1 Tbsp, roasted if desired
Red chillies	4
Pure coconut cream (*pati santan*)	squeezed from 1/2 grated coconut
Salt	1/2 tsp

Method

- Coarsely shred pineapple and set aside.
- Grind or blend (process) dried prawns and chillies together to combine. Set aside.
- Into a mixing bowl, put shredded pineapple and all remaining ingredients and mix well.
- Serve with white rice.

Nasi Himpit

Preparation: 10 minutes   Cooking: 20 minutes

Ingredients

Rice	2½ cups
Water	1.375 litres
Salt	¼ tsp
Screwpine (*pandan*) leaves	3, washed and knotted

Method

- Wash and drain rice, then add water. Stir in salt and put in screwpine leaves. Cook rice until done.
- Stir and mash cooked rice with a wooden spoon while still hot and moist.
- Transfer mashed rice to a 25 x 15-cm rectangular dish or tin fitted with a flat lid a little smaller than rim of dish or tin. Press lid firmly onto rice and place a heavy object on top to compress rice.
- Leave for 6 hours or overnight in the refrigerator. Cut into 2.5-cm cubes and serve with rendang tok (page 147) or any other *rendang* or *satay*.

Fried Sar Hor Fun with Cockles

Preparation: 20 minutes   Cooking: 7 minutes   Serves 3

Ingredients

Cockles	300 g
Prawns (shrimps)	150 g, peeled
Salt	½ tsp
Ground white pepper	as needed
Cooking oil	4 Tbsp
Garlic	3 cloves, peeled
Flat rice noodles (*hor fun*)	600 g, cut into 0.6-cm strips
Bean sprouts	150 g, tailed
Eggs	2
Water	4 Tbsp

Seasoning (combined)

Dark soy sauce	1 Tbsp
Light soy sauce	2 Tbsp

Method

- Prepare and pour boiling hot water over cockles and drain immediately. Extract flesh and set aside. Discard shells.
- Season prawns with salt and pepper. Set aside.
- Heat 3 Tbsp oil in a wok until smoking hot. Add garlic and prawns and stir-fry quickly over high heat.
- Add noodles and stir-fry for 1–2 minutes, then add bean sprouts and stir to mix.
- Add combined seasoning ingredients and fry for 1 minute.
- Push noodles to one side of wok and add 1 Tbsp oil. Crack in eggs and leave them for 30 seconds to set, then stir-fry together with noodles and bean sprouts.
- Sprinkle water over noodles and stir-fry at the same time. Lastly, add cockles and fry for 30 seconds.
- Serve hot, with a dash of pepper.

Ipoh Sar Hor Fun (Rice Noodle Soup)

Preparation: 20 minutes Cooking: 40 minutes Serves 5–6

Ingredients

Chicken	450 g, preferably thigh portion
Cooking oil	as needed
Garlic	4 cloves, peeled and minced
Freshwater prawns (shrimps)	600 g, large, unpeeled
Anchovy (*ikan bilis*) or fresh chicken stock	2 litres, boiling hot
Salt	3 tsp
Chinese (garlic) chives	90 g
Flat rice noodles (*hor fun*)	600 g, cut into 6-mm strips
Spring onions (scallions)	2, chopped
Ground white pepper	

Seasoning

Salt	1 tsp
Sesame oil	1/2 tsp
Ground white pepper	1/4 tsp
Cooking oil	1 dsp

Method

- Into a mixing bowl, put chicken and seasoning ingredients. Mix well and leave for 15 minutes.
- Steam chicken for 15 minutes or until cooked. When cool, cut into 1.25-cm thick slices and arrange on a serving dish.
- Heat sufficient oil in a wok and lightly brown garlic. Add prawns and stir-fry over high heat for 3 minutes or until just cooked.
- Pour boiling hot anchovy or chicken stock into wok and bring to the boil. Dish out prawns, peel and halve lengthways. Arrange prawns on a serving dish.
- Return prawn shells to boiling stock and simmer over very low heat for 10 minutes to extract prawn flavour.
- Strain stock and return to the boil. Add salt. Sustain stock at the boil over low heat.
- Meanwhile, half fill a saucepan with water and add 1 Tbsp oil. Bring to the boil, then scald Chinese chives. Remove and cut into 5-cm lengths. Arrange on serving dish.
- In the same water, scald rice noodles for 1–2 minutes. Drain well.
- To serve, put some rice noodles into individual serving bowls, then top with chicken and prawns. Ladle boiling stock over and serve hot sprinkled with spring onions, some chives and a dash of pepper.

Kuih Cara Berlauk (with Prawns)

Preparation: 20 minutes Cooking: 1 hour Makes 60 small *kuih cara*

Ingredients

Prawns (shrimps)	300 g, peeled and cut into small pieces
Salt	$^{1}/_{2}$ tsp
Ground white pepper	$^{1}/_{4}$ tsp
Cooking oil	2 Tbsp
Shallots	5, peeled and finely sliced
Red chillies	2, seeded and finely sliced
Spring onion (scallion)	1, chopped

Batter

Plain (all-purpose) flour	300 g
Coconut cream	440 ml, squeezed from 1 grated coconut with a little water added
Eggs	2
Salt	1 tsp

Garnishing

Red chillies	3
Spring onion (scallion)	1, chopped
Crisp-fried shallots	

Method

- Season prawns with salt and pepper. Leave for 15 minutes.
- Heat oil in a wok and lightly brown shallots. Drain and set aside for garnishing.
- Add prawns to wok and stir-fry for 2 minutes or until cooked. Add chillies and spring onion. Remove and leave to cool.
- Prepare batter. Sift flour into a small mixing bowl. Stir in coconut cream, a little at a time. Lightly beat eggs with a fork before mixing into batter with salt. Stir in cooled prawn mixture.
- Grease and heat *kuih cara* mould over very low heat. The mould looks like a tray of egg-shaped cups and has a snug-fitting lid.
- Into each cup, spoon 1 Tbsp prawn batter or enough to fill and cook for 8–10 minutes.
- Remove lid and garnish when batter is almost cooked. Remove completely cooked *kuih* with a small butter knife.

Kuih Cara Berlauk (with Meat)

Preparation: 30 minutes Cooking: 1 hour
Makes 40–45 *kuih cara*

Ingredients

Minced beef	300 g
Meat curry powder	3 Tbsp
Cooking oil	2 Tbsp
Onions	2, peeled and finely chopped
Salt	1 tsp

Batter

Plain (all-purpose) flour	300 g
Coconut cream	440 ml, squeezed from 1 grated coconut with a little water added
Eggs	2
Salt	1 tsp

Garnishing

Red chillies	3, seeded and finely sliced
Spring onion (scallion)	1, finely chopped

Method

- Season meat with curry powder. Set aside.
- Heat oil in a wok and lightly brown onions. Add meat and salt. Stir-fry until meat is cooked and dry, then dish out and set aside. To prevent meat from sticking to wok, sprinkle a little water whilst frying.
- Prepare batter. Sift flour into a small mixing bowl. Stir in coconut cream, a little at a time, until smooth. Lightly beat eggs with a fork, then mix into batter together with salt.
- Grease and heat a *kuih cara* mould with large cups over low heat. Spoon 1/2 Tbsp batter into each cup, then 1 tsp minced meat filling. Top with 1 Tbsp batter or enough to cover filling and cook for about 10 minutes.
- Garnish when *kuih cara* is almost cooked and remove cooked *kuih* with a small butter knife.

Note: *Kuih cara* moulds come in various sizes. For this recipe, you will need a mould with bigger egg-shaped cups to accommodate the filling.

Kuih Cara Manis

Preparation: 15 minutes Cooking: 1 hour Makes 60 *kuih cara*

Ingredients

Plain (all-purpose) flour	300 g
Coconut cream	440 ml, squeezed from 1 grated coconut with a little water added
Screwpine (*pandan*) juice	1 Tbsp
Green food colouring	2–3 drops
Salt	1/4 tsp
Eggs	2
Castor (superfine) sugar	

Method

- Sift flour into a small mixing bowl. Stir in coconut cream, a little at a time, together with screwpine juice, food colouring and salt. Lightly beat eggs with a fork and stir into flour mixture.
- Grease *kuih cara* mould with a little butter and heat over very low heat.
- Fill each cup with batter and cook for about 8 minutes.
- When *kuih cara* is more than half-cooked, sprinkle 1 tsp sugar evenly over each surface.
- When *kuih* pieces are completely cooked, remove with a small butter knife.

Note: Instead of spooning batter into each cup of the mould, which is time-consuming, transfer batter to a measuring jug with a beak. This way, batter can be poured easily and quickly into moulds without spillage.

To obtain screwpine juice easily, wash and cut 4–5 leaves into small pieces and blend with a little water. Strain to get clear juice.

Puteri Berendam

Preparation: 15 minutes   Cooking: 20 minutes

Ingredients

Coconut cream	375 ml, squeezed from 1 grated coconut with a little water added
Sugar	3 Tbsp
Salt	$^{1}/_{4}$ tsp
Plain (all-purpose) flour	$^{1}/_{2}$ Tbsp
Screwpine (*pandan*) leaves	3, washed and knotted
Glutinous Rice Balls*	1 recipe

Method

- Into a saucepan, put coconut cream, sugar, salt and flour. Stir to mix until smooth.
- Add screwpine leaves and bring to the boil, stirring continuously.
- Add prepared glutinous rice balls and simmer for a few minutes or until coconut cream thickens.
- Serve hot.

*Glutinous Rice Balls

Glutinous rice flour	150 g
Water	250 ml
Green food colouring	a few drops
Filling**	1 recipe

Method

- Sift glutinous rice flour into a bowl. Add water and knead, together with green food colouring, until firm dough results.
- Shape small marble-size balls from dough. Flatten each ball lightly and top with a teaspoonful of filling. Press edges together and reshape into small balls.
- Bring a half filled saucepan of water to the boil. Put in glutinous rice balls, a few at a time.
- As soon as the balls float to the surface, remove with a perforated ladle.

**Filling

Palm sugar (*gula Melaka*)	60 g, chopped
Water	65 ml
Salt	a pinch
Grated skinned coconut	120 g

Method

- Into a small saucepan, put palm sugar, water and salt. Cook over low heat, stirring, until palm sugar dissolves.
- Strain syrup into a wok. Add grated coconut and fry until evenly coated with palm syrup. Dish out and leave to cool.

Kelantan

Kelantan, the "land of lightning", is situated in the northeast of Peninsular Malaysia. The coastal beaches, which extend for miles, are famous for their shimmering white sand dotted here and there with serene fishing *kampungs* whose occupants are noted for their strong and varied cultural activities. The people here are predominantly Malay and their economic life centres around offshore fishing and *padi* growing further inland on low fertile plains.

Isolated from the west of the Malaysian peninsula by the main mountain range and by strong monsoon winds from the South China Sea which bring heavy rainfall at the end and beginning of the year, Kelantan has bred a tough, weathered people steeped in cultural heritage. Prominent cultural activities like the *makyung* and *menora* dance drama are exclusive to Kelantan. Of particular note, too, are the *wayang kulit*, or shadow play, and *bersilat*, the Malay art of self-defence.

The most famous handicrafts, which form the basis of many cottage industries, are the exquisite silverware, *kain songket*, with intricately woven gold and silver threads, and handprinted batik in beautiful chromatic designs. Top spinning (*main gasing*) and kite (*wau*) flying are two favourite pastimes which have been elevated by skilled craftsmanship. Both are gay and spellbinding spectacles.

As exotic as their handicrafts is Kelantanese food — aromatic, enlivened with chillies and lots of shallots, mildly spiced and slightly sweet. Their Nasi Dagang — a unique rice with a brownish tinge steamed with coconut milk, Ayam Percik and Kuzi Ayam are East Coast specials. Kelantanese cooking may be slightly sweet but sugar can always be omitted from some dishes if natural sweetness from meat and coconut is preferred.

Kuzi Ayam

Preparation: 40 minutes Cooking: 45 minutes

Ingredients

Chicken	1, about 1.5 kg, cut into 4–6 pieces
Saffron strands	a few, ground with 1 tsp water
Shallots	600 g, peeled, sliced and crisp-fried
Water	1 litre
Cooking oil	4 Tbsp
Sultanas	60 g
Ghee (clarified butter)	2 dsp
Tomato sauce (ketchup)	4 Tbsp
Salt	1 dsp
Almonds	20, roasted
Sugar	1 tsp

Ingredients to be ground

Coriander seeds (*ketumbar biji*)	1 Tbsp
Fennel seeds (*jintan manis biji*)	1 dsp
Cumin seeds (*jintan putih biji*)	1 dsp
White peppercorns	1 dsp
Mace (*aril buah pala*)	1 piece
Cardamoms (*buah pelaga*)	5
Cloves (*bunga cengkih*)	5
Ginger	2.5-cm knob, peeled
Cinnamon (*kayu manis*)	2.5-cm stick
Turmeric (*kunyit*)	2.5-cm knob, peeled
Galangal (*lengkuas*)	3 slices, peeled

Ingredients to be combined

Evaporated milk	1 large can (410 g)
Kalamansi limes (*limau kesturi*) juice	squeezed from 3 limes

Ingredients to be sliced

Shallots	5, peeled
Garlic	3 cloves, peeled

Method

- Wash and dry chicken, then rub with ground saffron. If saffron is unavailable, use a few drops of yellow colouring instead.
- Into a large mixing bowl, put crisp-fried shallot slices, ground and combined ingredients and water. Mix well and set aside.
- Heat oil in a wok. Fry sultanas for 1 minute, then remove and drain.
- Add half the ghee to wok and fry chicken for 15 minutes. Dish out and drain.
- Transfer oil from wok to a curry pot. Add remaining ghee and brown sliced ingredients.
- Add ingredients from mixing bowl, tomato sauce and salt. Bring to the boil, stirring frequently.
- Add half the fried sultanas, half the roasted almonds, and sugar. Simmer until mixture thickens.
- Add fried chicken and cook over moderate heat until gravy is thick and oil separates.
- Serve, if desired, sprinkled with remaining sultanas and almonds.

Solok Lada

Preparation: 20 minutes Cooking: 15 minutes

Ingredients

Red chillies	16, large
Spanish mackerel (*ikan tenggiri*)	180 g, meat only, cut into large cubes
Grated skinned coconut	150 g
Shallots	6, peeled
Sugar	1 tsp
Salt	as needed
Coconut milk	190 ml, squeezed from $^3/_4$ grated coconut with sufficient water added

Method

- Slit chillies lengthways with a sharp knife for stuffing. Carefully remove seeds and membranes. Soak in water for 15 minutes.
- Into a blender (food processor), put fish cubes, grated coconut and shallots. Blend until fine, then stir in sugar and salt.
- Mix well.
- Stuff each chilli with 1 tablespoonful fish mixture.
- Into a pot, put stuffed chillies, slit side up. Then, carefully pour in coconut milk mixed with a pinch of salt.
- Cover pot and simmer gently for 15 minutes or until cooked and almost dry.

Note: Serve solok lada with rice or nasi kerabu (page 179).

Daging Goreng Pengantin

Preparation: 1 hour Cooking: 1 hour 15 minutes

Ingredients

Beef	1 kg, cut into 5 x 2.5-cm pieces
Salt	as needed
Dried sour fruit (*asam gelugur*)	2 pieces
Cooking oil	6 Tbsp
Shallots	300 g, peeled and sliced
Dried chillies	30, coarsely ground
Pure coconut cream (*pati santan*)	335 ml, squeezed from $1^1/_2$ grated coconuts
Sugar	$1^1/_2$ tsp

Ingredients to be finely ground

Ginger	2.5 x 1.25-cm knob, peeled
Coriander seeds (*ketumbar biji*)	1 Tbsp

Method

- Into a large pot, put beef pieces, 2 tsp salt and dried sour fruit slices. Add enough water to cover meat, then secure lid and simmer for 1 hour. Alternatively, pressure cook for 35 minutes.
- When done, remove meat and drain in a colander until dry and cool. Lightly pound cooled meat with a pestle, then break meat into small pieces using fingers.
- Heat oil in a wok and brown shallot slices. Remove with a perforated ladle when crisp and drain.
- Remove oil from wok, leaving behind about 2 Tbsp. Fry ground ingredients and chillies over low heat until oil separates.
- Add all remaining ingredients and bring to a slow boil, then simmer until thick.
- Add meat and fry continuously for 40 minutes or until almost dry.
- Add crisp-fried shallot slices and fry over very low heat for 15 minutes more or until dry and meat is almost crisp.
- Remove and leave to cool on absorbent paper. When thoroughly cooled, store in an airtight container.

Note: Daging goreng pengantin can be stored for a couple of weeks to accompany and make a rice meal more appetising. Served on buttered toast and in sandwiches, they make tasty though quite 'un-Kelantanese' snacks.

Daging Masak Lawar

Preparation: 25 minutes Cooking: 15 minutes

Ingredients

Beef fillet	600 g
Grated skinned coconut	4–5 Tbsp, for *kerisik* (page 11), ground
Lime (*limau nipis*) juice	squeezed from 3 limes
Pure coconut cream (*pati santan*)	250 ml, squeezed from 1 grated coconut
Salt	1 1/2 tsp

Ingredients to be ground

Coriander seeds (*ketumbar biji*)	1 Tbsp, roasted
Red chillies	8
Shallots	16, peeled
Ginger	2.5-cm knob, peeled

Method

- Bring a saucepan half filled with water to the boil. Add beef and boil until cooked. Drain and slice cooled beef into thin 4-cm strips.
- Into a cooking pot, put *kerisik*, ground ingredients, lime juice, coconut cream and beef. Mix well, then bring to a slow boil.
- Reduce heat and simmer, stirring frequently, until gravy is thick. Add remaining ingredients.

Rendang Daging

Preparation: 20 minutes Cooking: 1 hour

Ingredients

Beef	1.5 kg, scored and cut into 5 x 2.5-cm pieces
Pure coconut cream (*pati santan*)	750 ml, squeezed from 3 grated coconuts
Coconut milk	750 ml, squeezed from same grated coconuts with sufficient water added
Kaffir lime leaves (*daun limau purut*)	4, finely sliced
Turmeric leaves (*daun kunyit*)	4, finely sliced
Dried sour fruit (*asam gelugur*)	3 pieces
Salt	2 tsp
Sugar	1 tsp

Ingredients to be ground

Red bird's eye chillies (*cili padi*)	15
Green bird's eye chillies (*cili padi*)	15
Shallots	300 g, peeled
Garlic	10 cloves, peeled
Ginger	5 x 2.5-cm knob, peeled
Galangal (*lengkuas*)	4 x 2.5-cm knob, peeled
Turmeric (*kunyit*)	5 x 2.5-cm, knob, peeled
Lemon grass (*serai*)	5 stalks

Method

- Into a mixing bowl, put meat and ground ingredients. Mix well and leave for 15 minutes.
- Into a pressure cooker, put beef and coconut milk. Cook for 30 minutes.
- At the end of that time, add coconut cream and bring to the boil.
- Reduce heat and simmer until gravy is almost thick.
- Add finely sliced leaves and dried sour fruit slices, then simmer, stirring continuously, until meat is tender and gravy thick.
- Add salt and sugar.

Daging Masak Merah

Preparation: 30 minutes   Cooking: 1 hour 15 minutes

Ingredients

Beef	600 g, scored and cut into 4-cm cubes
Cooking oil	6 Tbsp
Shallots	450 g, peeled and sliced
Cashew nuts	120 g
Sultanas	90 g
Dried chillies	40, soaked and ground
Water	1.25 litres
Jackfruit leaves (*daun nangka*)	2–3
Evaporated milk	1 large can (410 g)
Tomato purée	1/2 can (140 g)
Tomato sauce (ketchup)	4 Tbsp
Tamarind pulp (*asam Jawa*)	2 tsp, mixed with a little water and strained
Salt	2 tsp
Mint leaves	a few sprigs
Coriander leaves (cilantro)	2 sprigs, cut into 2.5-cm lengths
Spring onions (scallions)	2, cut into 2.5-cm lengths
Sugar	1 tsp

Ingredients to be ground

Ginger	5-cm knob, peeled
Turmeric (*kunyit*)	5-cm knob, peeled

Method

- Mix beef and ground ingredients together and leave aside.
- Heat oil and lightly brown shallot slices until crisp. Remove with a perforated ladle and set aside.
- Reheat oil and fry cashew nuts until lightly browned. Drain and set aside.
- Put in sultanas and fry for 1 minute, then remove and drain. Add ground chillies and fry until oil separates. Dish out.
- Add beef, water and jackfruit leaves. Bring to the boil, then reduce heat and simmer for 1 hour or until beef is tender.
- Discard jackfruit leaves and add all remaining ingredients, including those fried. Simmer, stirring frequently, until gravy is thick and meat tender.

Note: Jackfruit leaves are used as a meat tenderiser.

Roast Tongue

Preparation: 30 minutes   Cooking: 1 hour 15 minutes

Ingredients

Cow's tongue	1
Turmeric (*kunyit*)	5 x 2.5-cm knob, peeled and ground
Salt	as needed
Vinegar	1 dsp
Light soy sauce	2 dsp
Ground white pepper	1 dsp
Tapioca flour	3 Tbsp, mixed with a little water into a paste
Potatoes	3, peeled and halved

Garnishing (optional)

Spring onion (scallion)

Red chillies

Method

- Scald tongue in boiling water. Drain and scrape off skin with a knife.
- Prick tongue with a skewer, then rub with ground turmeric and 1 dsp salt. Leave for 15 minutes.
- Into a pressure cooker, put tongue and add enough water to cover and pressure cook for 45 minutes.
- When done, drain tongue and season with vinegar, soy sauce, pepper, salt and tapioca flour paste.
- Transfer tongue and seasoning to a baking dish and add potato halves.
- Roast in an oven preheated to 175°C/350°F for 30 minutes or until tongue is tender and potatoes cooked.
- Remove tongue and thinly slice. Arrange on a serving dish, with potatoes. Pour pan sauce over tongue slices.
- Serve garnished, if desired, with spring onion and chillies.

Ros Ayam

Preparation: 15 minutes Cooking: 40 minutes

Ingredients

Cooking oil for deep-frying

Chicken	1, about 1.5 kg, cut into 4–6 pieces
Water	1 litre
Shallots	15, peeled, sliced and crisp-fried
Garlic	5 cloves, peeled, sliced and crisp-fried
Evaporated milk	1 small can (170 g)
Potatoes	4, peeled and halved
Onions	3, peeled and cut into wedges
Chinese (garlic) chives	10 stalks, cut into 4-cm lengths
Red chillies	4, sliced
Salt	2 tsp or to taste

Method

- Heat oil for deep-frying in a wok. Deep-fry chicken for 10 minutes or until lightly browned. Drain and set aside.
- In a saucepan, bring water to the boil. Lower in fried chicken and return to the boil, then simmer over low heat for 10 minutes.
- Mix half the crisp-fried shallot and garlic slices into evaporated milk, then add to chicken. Return to the boil.
- Add potatoes and onions and simmer until chicken is tender.
- Mix in all remaining ingredients. Dish out and serve hot, sprinkled with remaining crisp-fried shallots and garlic.

Kelantanese Egg Curry

Preparation: 15 minutes Cooking: 30 minutes

Ingredients

Cooking oil	5 Tbsp
Coconut milk	1 litre, squeezed from 2 grated coconuts with sufficient water added
Dried sour fruit (*asam gelugur*)	4 pieces
Hard-boiled eggs	20, shelled
Tomatoes	6, cut into wedges
Red chillies	6, left whole
Green chillies	6, left whole
Salt	2½ tsp or to taste
Sugar	1 tsp

Ingredients to be sliced

Shallots	5, peeled
Garlic	5 cloves, peeled

Ingredients to be ground

Dried chillies	20, soaked
Ginger	4-cm knob, peeled
Galangal (*lengkuas*)	4-cm knob, peeled
Turmeric (*kunyit*)	4-cm knob, peeled
Lemon grass (*serai*)	4 stalks
White peppercorns	30
Coriander seeds (*ketumbar biji*)	2 Tbsp

Method

- Heat oil in a wok. Brown sliced ingredients.
- Add ground ingredients and fry until fragrant and oil separates.
- Add coconut milk and dried sour fruit slices. Bring to a slow boil.
- Add all remaining ingredients and return to the boil, then remove from heat.

Note: To shell hard-boiled eggs easily, add a little vinegar when boiling.

Kerabu Sotong Kering

Preparation: 20 minutes   Cooking: 1 minute

Ingredients

Dried cuttlefish shreds	90 g
Green mango	1, small, peeled, seeded and cut into strips
Cucumber	1/2, seed portion discarded then shredded
Red chillies	2, finely sliced
Bird's eye chillies (*cili padi*)	6, finely sliced
Shallots	7, peeled and finely sliced
Lime (*limau nipis*) juice	squeezed from 3–4 limes
Sugar	2 Tbsp or to taste
Cooking oil for deep-frying	

Method

- Wash and drain cuttlefish flakes. Then, dry them in the sun or in an oven preheated to 150°C/300°F.
- Meanwhile, combine all remaining ingredients, except oil, in a bowl.
- When well mixed, transfer to a colander and leave to drain for 1 hour.
- Heat oil for deep-frying in a wok. Deep-fry dried cuttlefish flakes until light golden and crisp. Drain and leave to cool.
- Just before serving, toss squid crisps with other ingredients to combine.
- Serve on a flat dish.

Note: Prepared shredded cuttlefish is sold in packets and easily obtainable in Kelantan and Terengganu.

Ayam Masak Keremak

Preparation: 20 minutes Cooking: 30 minutes

Ingredients

Chicken	1, about 1.5 kg, cut into bite-size pieces
Salt	as needed
Cooking oil	3 Tbsp
Ghee (clarified butter)	2 Tbsp
Shallots	20, peeled and sliced
Garlic	5 cloves, peeled
Coconut cream	250 ml, squeezed from 1 grated coconut with a little water added
Coconut milk	750 ml, squeezed from same grated coconut with sufficient water added
Red chillies	3, left whole
Green chillies	3, left whole
Tomatoes	3, halved
Evaporated milk	3 Tbsp
Lime (*limau nipis*) juice	squeezed from 1 lime

Ingredients to be ground

Coriander seeds (*ketumbar biji*)	3 Tbsp
Poppy seeds	3 Tbsp
Fennel seeds (*jintan manis biji*)	2 tsp
Cumin seeds (*jintan putih biji*)	2 tsp
Ground white pepper	2 tsp
Cashew nuts	10

Spices

Cinnamon (*kayu manis*)	1.25-cm stick
Cloves (*bunga cengkih*)	5
Cardamoms (*buah pelaga*)	5
Mace (*aril buah pala*)	3 pieces

Method

- Season chicken with ground ingredients and 1 1/2 tsp salt. Leave for 30 minutes.
- Heat oil and ghee in a curry pot. Lightly brown shallots and garlic.
- Add spices and fry until fragrant, then add chicken and stir-fry until almost dry.
- Pour in coconut milk and bring to the boil, then reduce heat and simmer for 15 minutes.
- Add chillies, tomatoes, coconut cream, evaporated milk and lime juice. Simmer for 5 minutes more.
- When meat is tender, add salt to taste.

Ayam Kerutuk

Preparation: 20 minutes Cooking: 40 minutes

Ingredients

Chicken	1, about 1.5 kg
Cooking oil	3 Tbsp
Shallots	10, peeled and sliced
Dried chillies	45 g, soaked and ground
Grated skinned coconut	4 Tbsp, for *kerisik* (page 11), ground
Dried sour fruit (*asam gelugur*)	2 pieces
Coconut milk	1 litre, squeezed from 1 grated coconut with sufficient water added
Sugar	1 tsp

Ingredients to be ground

Ground coriander (*ketumbar serbuk*)	2 Tbsp
Cardamoms (*buah pelaga*)	5
Cloves (*bunga cengkih*)	5
Fennel seeds (*jintan manis biji*)	1 tsp
Cumin seeds (*jintan putih biji*)	1 tsp
Black peppercorns	1 tsp
Cinnamon (*kayu manis*)	1.25-cm stick
Turmeric (*kunyit*)	4-cm knob, peeled
Galangal (*lengkuas*)	4-cm knob, peeled
Ginger	5 x 2.5-cm knob, peeled
Lemon grass (*serai*)	2 stalks
Garlic	5 cloves, peeled

Method

- Cut chicken into 4–8 pieces.
- Heat oil in a cooking pot. Fry shallots and half the ground chillies. Remove and set aside.
- In a mixing bowl, put *kerisik*, remaining ground chillies and ground ingredients. Add chicken pieces and mix well, then leave for 15 minutes.
- In a cooking pot, put seasoned chicken and dried sour fruit slices. Bring to a slow boil over medium heat, stirring gently.
- When pot's contents are semi-dry, pour in coconut milk. Return to the boil, then simmer over low heat, stirring constantly, for 15 minutes or until gravy is half-dry. Add fried shallots and chillies and seasoning.
- Allow to simmer for 20 minutes or until chicken is tender and oil separates.

Kerabu Perut

Preparation: 20 minutes Cooking: 1 hour

Ingredients

Tripe	1 kg
Salt	as needed
Grated skinned coconut	5 Tbsp, for *kerisik* (page 11), coarsely ground
Shallots	10, peeled and sliced
Red chillies	5, seeded and sliced
Polygonum leaves (*daun kesum*)	1 small bunch, finely sliced
Lime (*limau nipis*) juice	squeezed from 3 limes
Grated skinned coconut	3 Tbsp
Sugar	1 tsp
Pure coconut cream (*pati santan*)	125 ml, squeezed from 1/2 grated coconut

Method

- Clean tripe and rub with some salt, then boil in a saucepan of water until tender.
- Drain tripe and slice into 1.25-cm wide strips.
- Put tripe pieces into a mixing bowl. Except coconut cream, add all remaining ingredients and mix well.
- Add coconut cream only just before serving.

Solo Itik

Preparation: 30 minutes Cooking: 1 hour 15 minutes

Ingredients

Duck	1, about 1.5 kg
Turmeric (*kunyit*)	15 x 2.5-cm knob, peeled and ground
Salt	as needed
Lemon grass (*serai*)	6 stalks, lightly crushed
Ginger	15 x 2.5-cm knob, peeled and lightly crushed
Cinnamon (*kayu manis*)	10-cm stick
Cloves (*bunga cengkih*)	7
Cardamoms (*buah pelaga*)	8
Grated skinned coconut	2 Tbsp, for *kerisik* (page 11), coarsely ground
Coconut cream	625 ml, squeezed from 2 grated coconuts with a little water added
Rice flour	2 Tbsp, mixed with 125 ml water or coconut milk until smooth
Shallots	10, peeled, sliced and crisp-fried, lightly crushed
Sugar cane	1 stick, about 90-cm long

Ingredients to be ground

Coriander seeds (*ketumbar biji*)	1 Tbsp
Fennel seeds (*jintan manis biji*)	1 tsp
Cumin seeds (*jintan putih biji*)	1 tsp
Cloves (*bunga cengkih*)	3
Cardamoms (*buah pelaga*)	2
Mace (*aril buah pala*)	2 pieces
Black peppercorns	10
Dried chillies	20, soaked
Shallots	30, peeled
Galangal (*lengkuas*)	5-cm knob, peeled
Ginger	2.5-cm knob, peeled

Garnishing

Lettuce

Cucumber

Chillies

Method

- Wash and clean duck thoroughly, then rub with ground turmeric and 2 tsp salt. Leave for 15 minutes.
- Rinse duck under a running tap. Stitch up openings of duck, leaving 2.5 cm at the neck and the end for sugar cane stick to go through.
- Into a large pot, put duck, lemon grass, ginger, cinnamon, cloves and cardamoms. Add enough water to cover duck and bring to a slow boil.
- Reduce heat and simmer for 45 minutes or until duck is just tender. Remove pot from heat and drain duck.
- Reserve 2 Tbsp ground ingredients. In a saucepan, mix remaining ground ingredients with *kerisik*, coconut cream, rice flour batter and 1 tsp salt. Bring to a slow boil.
- Reduce heat and simmer, stirring continuously, until gravy is thick. Stir in crisp-fried shallot slices. If short of time, this basting gravy can be prepared a day ahead and refrigerated.
- To barbecue duck, make 3 diagonal slits across back and breast of duck with a sharp knife. Rub reserved ground ingredients all over and leave for 15 minutes. Allow duck to cool thoroughly.
- Thread cooled duck through sugar cane stick, then spoon thickened gravy over.
- Barbecue duck over glowing charcoal pit, rotating sugar cane stick to brown duck evenly. Repeat basting twice and cook until duck is done.
- Remove duck from stick, then garnish and serve hot.

Nasi Kerabu

Preparation: 40 minutes Cooking: 45 minutes Serves 8

Ingredients

Chubb mackerels (*ikan kembung*)	2–3, grilled and flaked
Skinned coconut	1, grated, for *kerisik* (page 11)
Salt	1/2 tsp
Sugar	1 tsp
Cooked rice	sufficient for 8 persons
Coconut Sauce*	1 recipe
Side Dish**	1 recipe

Ingredients to be ground

Shallots	8, peeled
Ginger	2.5-cm knob, peeled
Ground white pepper	1/4 tsp

Garnishing

Cucumber	1, shredded
Polygonum leaves (*daun kesum*)	5–6 sprigs, finely sliced
Long (snake) beans	6, finely sliced
Lemon grass (*serai*)	2 stalks, finely sliced
Young cashew nut leaves	10, finely sliced

Method

- Into a mixing bowl, put flaked fish, ground ingredients and *kerisik*. Add salt and sugar and mix well. Transfer to a serving dish.
- Arrange garnishing ingredients attractively on another serving dish.
- To serve nasi kerabu, first put some rice onto individual serving plates, then pile on desired amounts of flaked fish, coconut sauce and garnishing ingredients. Mix well with rice.
- Serve with Side Dish.

*Coconut Sauce

Dried chillies	10, soaked
Shallots	8, peeled
Coconut milk	1 litre, squeezed from 1 grated coconut with sufficient water added
Dried sour fruit (*asam gelugur*)	2 pieces
Lemon grass (*serai*)	2 stalks, lightly crushed
Sugar	1 tsp
Salt	1 tsp

Method

- Combine dried chillies and shallots by grinding or blending (processing) in a blender.
- Into a pot, put coconut milk, ground chillies and shallots, dried sour fruit slices and lemon grass. Bring to a slow boil.
- Simmer gently, stirring constantly, for 10 minutes or until oil separates.
- Add sugar and salt, then transfer to a serving bowl.

**Side Dish

Chubb mackerels (*ikan kembung*)	8, small–medium
Salt	1 tsp
Tamarind pulp (*asam Jawa*)	1 tsp, mixed with 2 Tbsp water and strained
Cooking oil	

Batter

Rice flour	1 cup
Water	125 ml
Ground turmeric (*kunyit*)	1/2 tsp
Salt	a pinch

Method

- Rub fish with salt and tamarind juice. Leave for 15 minutes.
- Meanwhile, prepare batter. Combine all ingredients and blend until smooth.
- Dip seasoned fish into batter and fry in hot oil for 2–3 minutes on each side.
- When cooked through and light golden, drain fish and transfer to a serving dish.

Taihi Itik

Preparation: 5 minutes   Cooking: 15 minutes

Ingredients

Egg whites	5
Sugar	180 g
Plain (all-purpose) flour	1 1/2 tsp
Screwpine (*pandan*) leaves	2, washed and knotted
Cloves (*bunga cengkih*)	4

Method

- Through a fine sieve, strain egg whites into a mixing bowl.
- Stir in sugar and flour. Continue stirring until sugar is dissolved. Transfer mixture to a small saucepan.
- Add to saucepan screwpine leaves and cloves, then cook over low heat, stirring with a wooden spoon, until dry and mixture is of custard consistency.
- Serve hot or cold, spread on toast.

Jemput Durian

Preparation: 10 minutes   Cooking: 5 minutes
Makes 20

Ingredients

Egg	1
Sugar	15 g
Salt	1/4 tsp
Water or milk	125 ml
Durian pulp	180 g, from 1 small durian
Cooking oil for deep-frying	

Ingredients to be sifted together

Self-raising flour	90 g
Baking powder	1 tsp
Cornflour (cornstarch)	30 g

Method

- Whisk egg and sugar until light and fluffy.
- Add salt and fold in sifted ingredients alternately with water or milk.
- Add durian pulp and mix well.
- Heat oil for deep-frying in a wok. Fry tablespoonfuls of batter over very low heat until dark brown. Drain well before serving.

Nasi Dagang

Preparation: 15 minutes   Cooking: 1 hour

Ingredients

Nasi Dagang rice (*beras lembut*)	4 cups
Pure coconut cream (*pati santan*)	375 ml, squeezed from 1 1/2 grated coconuts
Coconut milk	375 ml, squeezed from same grated coconuts with sufficient water added
Shallots	10, peeled and sliced
Ginger	2.5-cm knob, peeled and shredded
Fenugreek seeds (*halba*)	1/4 tsp
Salt	1 tsp

Method

- Wash rice and soak in water overnight.
- On cooking day, drain rice and steam for 30 minutes.
- Stir in coconut milk and steam for 15 minutes or until rice is nearly cooked.
- In a mixing bowl, combine all remaining ingredients and stir into cooked rice. Steam for 15 minutes more or until rice is properly cooked.

Note: *Beras lembut* is a special rice for nasi dagang and it has a brownish tinge. If *beras lembut* is unavailable, substitute with 700 g good grade Thai rice combined with 240 g glutinous rice.

Laksa Kelantan

Preparation: 30 minutes Cooking: 40 minutes Serves approximately 10

Ingredients

Chubb mackerels (*ikan kembung*)	1 kg
Salt	as needed
Coconut milk	2.125 litres, squeezed from 1 grated coconut with sufficient water added
Polygonum leaves (*daun kesum*)	10 sprigs
Torch ginger bud (*bunga kantan*)	1, split
Dried sour fruit (*asam gelugur*)	4 pieces
Sugar	1 tsp
Fresh thick round rice (*laksa*) noodles	$1\frac{1}{2}$ packets (750 g), scalded in boiling water and drained

Ingredients to be ground

Dried chillies	15, soaked
Galangal (*lengkuas*)	2.5-cm knob, peeled
Ginger	1.25-cm knob, peeled
Turmeric (*kunyit*)	2.5-cm knob, peeled
Black peppercorns	1 tsp

Ingredients to be sliced

Shallots	15, peeled
Garlic	3 cloves, peeled

Garnishing

Cucumbers	2, peeled, soft centres discarded and shredded
Bean sprouts	300 g, tailed and scalded
Long (snake) beans	8, cut into 2.5-cm lengths and scalded
Polygonum leaves (*daun kesum*)	5–6 sprigs, stalks discarded and leaves washed
Torch ginger bud (*bunga kantan*)	1, sliced
Mint leaves	1 small bunch
Basil leaves	1 small bunch

Method

- Season fish with 2 tsp salt and leave for 15 minutes.
- Steam and flake fish, then blend coarsely with coconut milk, one third at a time. Transfer blended mixture to a cooking pot.
- Add to pot ground and sliced ingredients. Bring to the boil, then reduce heat and simmer for 10 minutes.
- Except noodles and garnishing, add all remaining ingredients. Simmer for 20 minutes, stirring frequently.
- To serve, put some noodles into individual serving bowls. Top with a little of each garnishing ingredient and ladle hot fish gravy over. Serve hot.

Note: Do not throw away the torch ginger stems. Instead, lightly smash them and add to gravy during simmering. Discard when gravy is ready to be served.

Ayam Percik

Preparation: 15 minutes   Cooking: 10 minutes   Grilling: 15–20 minutes

Ingredients

Chicken	1, about 1.5 kg, cut into 4 large pieces
Salt	as needed
Coconut milk	750 ml, squeezed from 1 1/2 grated coconuts with sufficient water added
Rice flour	1 rounded (heaped) Tbsp
Tamarind pulp (*asam Jawa*)	1 Tbsp, mixed with 4 Tbsp water and strained
Sugar	1 tsp

Ingredients to be ground (A)

Ginger	2.5-cm knob, peeled
Garlic	4 cloves, peeled

Ingredients to be ground (B)

Dried chillies	8, soaked
Shallots	8, peeled
Ginger	1.25-cm knob, peeled
Dried prawn (shrimp) paste (*belacan*)	2.5-cm square piece

Method

- Season chicken pieces with ground ingredients (A) and 1 tsp salt.
- Leave for 1 hour.
- Into a cooking pot, put coconut milk, rice flour, ground ingredients (B) and tamarind juice. Bring to a slow boil.
- Add 1 tsp salt and sugar and keep stirring over low heat for 10 minutes or until liquid is thickened.
- Dip chicken pieces into thick coconut gravy and place over glowing charcoal grill.
- Baste chicken frequently with coconut gravy while grilling, takes about 15 minutes for chicken to cook through and brown evenly on both sides.

Terengganu

Unspoilt beauty, refreshing and unhurried, gentle and tranquil with long stretches of sparkling white, palm-fringed beaches: these are some of the attributes of Terengganu.

The idyllic coastline abounds with quaint, peaceful fishing villages, the mastery of their craftsmen reflected in the intricate *bangaus* (mastheads) of skillfully carved boats.

Apart from access to the sea, a rich fishing ground for local fishermen, the beaches in this vicinity are reputed to be the most rewarding for turtle-watching when turtles make their trek up the beach to lay eggs, a ritual occurring every year around August.

As in Kelantan, the people of Terengganu are well-known for their handicrafts, like silk and *songket* weaving, brassware metalworking and *mengkuang* weaving, all of which make up their cottage industries.

In Terengganu, one should not fail to experience Malay cuisine which is unique to the East Coast. Their Ayam Percik, which is grilled, is popular and the style of cooking shows a Thai influence. Nasi Ulam — a dish of rice mixed with a variety of finely cut tender shoots and vegetables and accompanied by a coconut *sambal* (chilli paste) — and their highly spiced Daging Kerutut Kering and Beef Rendang are just samples of tempting dishes which are as reputable as their *wayang kulit* (shadow puppetry) and sinuous kris.

Sambal Ikan Kembung

Preparation: 20 minutes   Cooking: 1 hour 5 minutes

Ingredients

Chubb mackerels (*ikan kembung*)	1 kg, or horse mackerel (*ikan cupak*)
Pure coconut cream (*pati santan*)	375 ml, squeezed from $1^{1}/_{2}$ grated coconuts
Dried sour fruit (*asam gelugur*)	2 large pieces
Salt	2 tsp
Sugar	2 tsp

Ingredients to be ground

Red chillies	15
Ginger	4-cm knob, peeled
Shallots	15, peeled
Garlic	2 cloves, peeled

Method

- Steam cleaned fish for 12 minutes or until cooked. When cool, remove bones and lightly mash flesh with the back of a spoon.
- Into a pan, put coconut cream and ground ingredients. Then, mix in all remaining ingredients, including mashed fish.
- Bring mixture to a slow boil over moderate heat, stirring frequently, takes about 5 minutes.
- When liquid reaches the boil, reduce heat and fry continuously for about 50 minutes, taking care mixture does not stick to pan, until completely dry.

Note: Sambal ikan kembung is like meat floss and is quite crisp out of the pan.

Beef Rendang, Terengganu Style

Preparation: 20 minutes Cooking: 1 hour 15 minutes

Ingredients

Beef	600 g, cut into 5 x 0.6-cm slices
Coconut milk	1.25 litres, squeezed from 2 grated coconuts with sufficient water added
Turmeric leaf (*daun kunyit*)	1, large
Kaffir lime leaf (*daun limau purut*)	1, sliced
Grated skinned coconut	120 g, for *kerisik* (page 11)

Ingredients to be ground

Dried chillies	25, soaked
Shallots	16, peeled
Garlic	2 cloves, peeled
Lemon grass (*serai*)	2 stalks, sliced
Ginger	1.25-cm knob, peeled
Galangal (*lengkuas*)	1.25-cm knob, peeled

Method

- Into a mixing bowl, put beef and ground ingredients. Mix well and leave for 15 minutes.
- Into a wok, pour coconut milk and add seasoned beef. Mix well and bring to a slow boil over medium heat, stirring occasionally.
- Reduce heat and simmer for 1 hour, stirring frequently, until gravy is thick.
- Add leaves and *kerisik*, then stir continuously for 15 minutes or until very little gravy remains.

Daging Kerutut Kering

Preparation: 25 minutes Cooking: 50 minutes to 1 hour

Ingredients

Beef	1 kg, or 1.5 kg chicken
Cooking oil	4 Tbsp
Onion	1, peeled and sliced
Cinnamon (*kayu manis*)	1.25-cm stick
Cardamoms (*buah pelaga*)	2
Cloves (*bunga cengkih*)	3
Coconut milk	750 ml, squeezed from 1 grated coconut with sufficient water added
Dried sour fruit (*asam gelulgur*)	2 pieces
Sugar	1 rounded (heaped) tsp
Screwpine (*pandan*) leaves	3, washed and knotted
Grated skinned coconut	4 Tbsp, for *kerisik* (page 11)
Salt	2 tsp

Ingredients to be ground

Dried chillies	20, soaked
Shallots	12, peeled
Garlic	4 cloves, peeled
Turmeric (*kunyit*)	2.5-cm knob, peeled
Ginger	1.25-cm knob, peeled
Coriander seeds (*ketumbar biji*)	2 heaped Tbsp
Fennel seeds (*jintan manis biji*)	2 tsp
Cumin seeds (*jintan putih biji*)	1 tsp
Cinnamon (*kayu manis*)	1.25-cm stick
Star anise (*bunga lawang*)	2 sections
Cardamoms (*buah pelaga*)	3
Cloves (*bunga cengkih*)	3
Black peppercorns	12

Method

- Cut beef across grain into thin, 4-cm wide slices. If using chicken, cut into 8 pieces. Set aside.
- Heat oil in a wok until hot. Fry onion, cinnamon, cardamoms and cloves until fragrant, then add ground ingredients and fry over moderate heat until fragrant and oil separates. Add meat and continue frying for 3 minutes. Then, add coconut milk, dried sour fruit, sugar and screwpine leaves.
- Simmer over low heat, stirring frequently, for 40 minutes or until meat is tender and gravy thick. Add *kerisik* and salt. Stir-fry until very little gravy remains.
- Discard dried sour fruit and screwpine leaves before serving.

Ayam Terutuk

Preparation: 20 minutes Cooking: 40 minutes

Ingredients

Chicken	1, about 1.5 kg
Coconut milk	750 ml, squeezed from 1 grated coconut with sufficient water added
Grated skinned coconut	4 Tbsp, for *kerisik* (page 11)
Tamarind pulp (*asam Jawa*)	1 Tbsp, mixed with 65 ml water and strained
Sugar	1 tsp
Salt	2 tsp or to taste

Ingredients to be ground

Dried chillies	35, soaked
Garlic	3 cloves, peeled
Shallots	12, peeled
Galangal (*lengkuas*)	2.5-cm knob, peeled
Turmeric (*kunyit*)	2.5-cm knob, peeled
Ginger	1.25-cm knob, peeled
Coriander seeds (*ketumbar biji*)	2 Tbsp
Fennel seeds (*jintan manis biji*)	1 Tbsp
Cloves (*bunga cengkih*)	4
Cardamoms (*buah pelaga*)	4

Method

- Cut chicken into 8 pieces and drain in a colander.
- Into a pot, put coconut milk, ground ingredients and *kerisik*. Bring to the boil.
- Stir in tamarind juice, then add chicken. Cook over low heat, stirring frequently, until chicken is tender and gravy thickens.
- Add sugar and salt to taste.

Ayam Percik

Preparation: 30 minutes Cooking: 15 minutes Grilling: 30 minutes

Ingredients

Chicken	1, about 1.5 kg, cut into 6–8 pieces
Black peppercorns	1 rounded (heaped) tsp, ground
Salt	1 1/2 rounded (heaped) tsp
Cooking oil	3 Tbsp
Pure coconut cream (*pati santan*)	625 ml, squeezed from 2 grated coconuts
Light soy sauce	1 tsp

Ingredients to be ground

Shallots	20, peeled
Candlenuts (*buah keras*)	5
Coriander seeds (*ketumbar biji*)	1 Tbsp
Fennel seeds (*jintan manis biji*)	1 tsp
Cumin seeds (*jintan putih biji*)	1 tsp
Lemon grass (*serai*)	3 stalks
Galangal (*lengkuas*)	5-cm knob, peeled

Method

- Season chicken pieces with ground black peppercorns and 1 tsp salt. Leave for at least 1 hour.
- Heat oil in a wok and fry ground ingredients until fragrant.
- Add coconut cream, 1/2 tsp salt and light soy sauce. Simmer over low heat for 8–10 minutes or until thick and oil separates.
- Drain chicken pieces and coat with thickened gravy. Then, place on prepared charcoal grill.
- As chicken pieces cook, baste frequently with more gravy. Remove when cooked through.
- Serve with white rice or nasi minyak (page 194) and a cucumber salad, if desired.

Note: Ayam percik tastes very much like ayam satay (page 26).

Ayam Golek

Preparation: 15 minutes   Cooking: 30 minutes   Baking: 30 minutes

Ingredients

Chicken	1, about 1.5 kg
Salt	3 tsp
Coconut milk	750 ml, squeezed from 1 grated coconut with sufficient water added
Red chillies (optional) for garnishing	

Ingredients to be ground

Shallots	12, peeled
Garlic	3 cloves, peeled
Lemon grass (*serai*)	3 stalks
Galangal (*lengkuas*)	5-cm knob, peeled
Ginger	2.5-cm knob, peeled
White peppercorns	1 tsp
Cumin seeds (*jintan putih biji*)	1 tsp
Fennel seeds (*jintan manis biji*)	1 Tbsp

Method

- Rub chicken with 2 tsp salt and set aside.
- Into a wok, put coconut milk and ground ingredients. Bring to a slow boil.
- Add chicken and all remaining ingredients. Simmer over low heat for 30 minutes, turning chicken halfway through cooking.
- When gravy thickens, transfer chicken and gravy to a heatproof oven dish.
- Bake chicken in an oven preheated to 175°C/350°F for 30 minutes or until chicken is cooked through and lightly browned.
- Serve hot, garnished with red chillies, if desired.

Rojak Betik Terengganu

Preparation: 30 minutes   Cooking: 10 minutes

Ingredients

Half-ripe papaya	$^{1}/_{2}$, small, peeled and shredded
Bean sprouts	240 g, scalded
Pineapple	$^{1}/_{2}$, peeled, quartered and sliced
Cucumber	$^{1}/_{2}$, halved and sliced

Sauce

Chubb mackerels (*ikan kembung*)	3, grilled and flaked
Dried chillies	20, soaked
Dried prawn (shrimp) paste (*belacan*)	2.5 x 1.25-cm piece
Palm sugar (*gula Melaka*)	60 g
Water	250 ml
Tamarind pulp (*asam Jawa*)	1 Tbsp
Vinegar	1 dsp
Salt	1 tsp or to taste

Method

- Combine shredded papaya and bean sprouts and transfer to a serving dish.
- Top with pineapple and cucumber slices. Set aside.
- Prepare sauce. Grind flaked fish, dried chillies and dried prawn paste together.
- When done, transfer to a mixing bowl and set aside.
- Into a saucepan, put palm sugar and water. Bring to the boil and cook over low heat until sugar dissolves. Add tamarind pulp and mix well, then strain liquid.
- Pour strained liquid over ground ingredients and mix well with vinegar and salt to taste.
- Just before serving, pour sauce over prepared vegetables.

Kurma Ayam

Preparation: 30 minutes Cooking: 30 minutes

Ingredients

Chicken	1, about 1.5 kg
Tomato sauce (ketchup)	180 g, or 1/2 bottle
Evaporated milk	1 large can (410 g)
Shallots	15, peeled, sliced, crisp-fried and lightly crushed
Cooking oil	4 Tbsp
Onion	1, peeled and sliced
Screwpine (*pandan*) leaves	2, washed and knotted
Salt	2 tsp

Ingredients to be ground

Shallots	12, peeled
Garlic	3 cloves, peeled
Ginger	1.25-cm knob, peeled
Coriander seeds (*ketumbar biji*)	1 Tbsp
Fennel seeds (*jintan manis biji*)	2 Tbsp
Poppy seeds	1 Tbsp

Spices

Cinnamon (*kayu manis*)	2.5-cm stick
Cardamoms (*buah pelaga*)	5
Cloves (*bunga cengkih*)	5

Method

- Cut chicken into bite-size pieces. Set aside.
- Prepare marinade. Into a mixing bowl, put tomato sauce, evaporated milk, crisp-fried shallot slices and ground ingredients.
- Mix in chicken pieces and leave to marinate for 30 minutes.
- Heat oil in a wok. Fry onion slices and spices until fragrant.
- Add chicken pieces and marinade. Bring to a slow boil.
- Add screwpine leaves and salt. Simmer over low heat for 25 minutes or until chicken is tender.

Nasi Minyak

Preparation: 15 minutes Cooking: 25 minutes

Ingredients

Rice	450 g
Ghee (clarified butter)	4 Tbsp
Shallots	6, peeled and sliced
Garlic	2 cloves, peeled and sliced
Ginger	1.25-cm knob, peeled and shredded
Water	690 ml
Screwpine (*pandan*) leaves	3, washed and knotted
Evaporated milk	3 Tbsp
Salt	1 rounded (heaped) tsp

Spices

Cinnamon (*kayu manis*)	2.5-cm stick
Cloves (*bunga cengkih*)	3
Cardamoms (*buah pelaga*)	3
Star anise (*bunga lawang*)	2 sections

Garnishing

Raisins	90 g
Crisp-fried shallots	

Method

- Wash and drain rice, then transfer to a rice cooker.
- Heat ghee in a wok. Add shallots, garlic, ginger and spices. Fry until fragrant.
- Except garnishing, add all remaining ingredients.
- Stir well and bring to the boil.
- Pour contents of wok into rice cooker. Cook until rice is done.
- Garnish and serve hot.

Kuih Belimbing

Preparation: 15 minutes Cooking: 20 minutes
Makes approximately 40

Ingredients

Plain (all-purpose) flour	150 g
Salt	a pinch
Butter	60 g
Water	190 ml
Eggs	2
Vanilla essence (extract)	1/2 tsp
Cooking oil for deep-frying	
Syrup*	1 recipe

Method

- Sift flour into a mixing bowl and add salt.
- In a saucepan, heat butter and water. When liquid reaches the boil, immediately pour into flour.
- Beat contents of mixing bowl until paste becomes a ball. Allow to cool slightly.
- Beat in eggs and vanilla essence. Resulting mixture should be a little stiff and hold its shape when piped.
- Fit a cookie press with a star nozzle, then pipe 5-cm lengths of mixture into hot oil.
- Stir kuih belimbing as they float up to brown evenly. Drain on absorbent paper.
- Arrange cooked *kuih* on a serving dish and just before serving, pour syrup over.

*Syrup

Sugar	120 g
Water	250 ml

Method

- In a small saucepan, combine sugar and water. Bring to the boil.
- Leave to cool before pouring over fried *kuih belimbing*.

Sri Kaya Peringi

Preparation: 30 minutes Cooking: 40 minutes

Ingredients

Pumpkin	1, medium, about 3 kg and 23–25.5-cm in diameter
Palm sugar (*gula Melaka*)	300 g, finely chopped
Water	65 ml
Eggs	7
Pure coconut cream (*pati santan*)	440 ml, squeezed from 1½ grated coconuts
Screwpine (*pandan*) juice	1 dsp

Method

- Wash pumpkin and carefully cut a circle, 10–12.5 cm in diameter, from the top. Peel top circle and set aside.
- Using a spoon, remove pumpkin seeds and membranes to leave a hollow case.
- Cut pumpkin flesh, from both hollow and top circle, into neat 1.25-cm cubes. When done, put pumpkin cubes into pumpkin case.
- In a small saucepan, combine palm sugar and water. Cook over low heat, stirring, until sugar dissolves. Strain and set aside.
- In a mixing bowl, lightly stir eggs with coconut cream, then add screwpine juice and palm sugar syrup. Mix well.
- Strain coconut cream mixture into pumpkin case. Stir mixture, then place pumpkin case into a large steamer already prepared for use.
- Steam for 35–40 minutes or until pumpkin is cooked.
- Serve soft custard hot or cold in small bowls.

Nasi Ulam

Preparation: 30 minutes Cooking: 30 minutes

Ingredients

Chubb mackerels (*ikan kembung*)	3, grilled, flaked and ground
Skinned coconut	$^1/_2$, grated, for *kerisik* (page 11)
Lime (*limau nipis*) juice	squeezed from 1 lime
Salt	1 tsp
Cooked rice	sufficient for 8 persons
*Sambal**	1 recipe

Ingredients to be finely sliced

Turmeric leaves (*daun kunyit*)	5
Polygonum leaves (*daun kesum*)	4 sprigs
Basil leaves (*daun kemangi*)	4 sprigs
Thai sweet basil leaves (*daun selasih*)	5 sprigs
Watercress	4 stalks
Lesser galangal leaves (*daun cekur*)	3
Kaffir lime leaves (*daun limau purut*)	3
Chinese lettuce leaves	3
Cashew nut leaves	4
Lemon grass (*serai*)	2 stalks, use only the tender central portion
Shallots	6, peeled
Torch ginger bud (*bunga kantan*)	1
Green chillies	3

Method

- In a mixing bowl, combine ground fish, *kerisik* and all finely sliced ingredients.
- Heat a dry wok until it is hot, then turn off heat.
- Add in combined ingredients, lime juice and salt. Mix well and transfer to a serving dish.
- To serve nasi ulam, ladle rice onto individual serving plates and top with desired amounts of combined ingredients and Sambal. Mix well.

**Sambal*

Coconut cream	250 ml, squeezed from 1 grated coconut with a little water added
Lemon grass (*serai*)	1 stalk, lightly crushed
Salt	$^1/_4$ tsp
Tamarind pulp (*asam Jawa*)	1 tsp, mixed with 2 Tbsp water and strained

Ingredients to be ground

Red chillies	10
Shallots	5, peeled
Ginger	1.25-cm knob, peeled

Method

- In a pot, combine coconut cream and ground ingredients.
- Add lemon grass, salt and tamarind juice.
- Simmer over low heat, stirring frequently, until sauce is thick and oil separates.

Penang

Penang is very often referred to as the "Pearl of the Orient". This exotic sun-splashed island boasts some of the finest beaches in Malaysia. One of the former British Straits Settlements, Penang was a prosperous trading post and entrepôt centre and its population became very cosmopolitan with indigenous Malays and an influx of immigrant Chinese, Indians and Arabs.

Malay curries show an Indian influence, though they are not as pungent as authentic Indian curries. There are local preparations of Kurma, Dalca and Crab Curry.

Highly popular Nyonya food, a delicious hybrid of Chinese and Malay cuisines, has its own flavours owing to the frequent use of ginger, galangal, lemon grass and dried prawn paste. The Nyonyas love a sour tang to their food and this is provided by the juice of tamarind pulp, dried sour fruit slices or tiny acidic fruit called blimbing, or *belimbing* in Malay. Nyonya favourites are Penang Laksa, Penang Acar, Curry Kapitan, Roti Jala, Otak-Otak Pulau Pinang and a host of enticing curries.

Indian Fish Curry with Bitter Gourd

Preparation: 15 minutes Cooking: 15 minutes

Ingredients

Black pomfret (*ikan bawal hitam*)	1, medium, cut into slices
Salt	as needed
Cooking oil	3 Tbsp
Garlic	5 cloves, peeled and sliced
Onions	2, peeled and sliced
Curry leaves	3 sprigs, stems discarded
Fenugreek seeds (*halba*)	1 tsp
Fish curry powder	2 rounded (heaped) Tbsp, mixed with 65 ml water
Tamarind pulp (*asam Jawa*)	2 Tbsp, mixed with 4 Tbsp water and strained
Coconut cream	250 ml, squeezed from 1 grated coconut with a little water added
Coconut milk	750 ml, squeezed from same grated coconut with sufficient water added
Bitter gourd	1, seeds and membranes scraped off, cut into 4-cm pieces and soaked in salted water
Sugar	1 tsp to taste

Ingredients to be ground

Ginger	2.5-cm knob, peeled
Turmeric (*kunyit*)	2.5-cm knob, peeled

Method

- Season fish with 1 tsp salt and leave for 15 minutes.
- Heat oil in a wok. Brown garlic and onions.
- Add curry leaves, fenugreek seeds and ground ingredients. Fry for a few minutes.
- Add curry paste and fry until fragrant. Then, pour in tamarind juice and coconut milk and bring to the boil.
- Add bitter gourd and simmer for 5 minutes, then put in fish. Simmer until fish is cooked and bitter gourd tender.
- Add coconut cream, salt and sugar to taste.

Penang Acar

Preparation: 45 minutes   Cooking: 20 minutes

Ingredients

Cucumbers	1.25 kg, halved lengthwise, seed portions discarded and cut into 4-cm long strips
Carrot	1, scraped and cut into 4-cm long strips
Salt	as needed
Vinegar	380 ml
Long (snake) beans	300 g, cut into 4-cm lengths
Cabbage	600 g, cut into 2.5-cm pieces
Red chillies	4, halved lengthwise, seeded and cut into thin strips
Cooking oil	500 ml
Sugar	180 g
Peanuts	600 g, roasted and coarsely ground

Ingredients to be ground (A)

Dried chillies	20, soaked
Red chillies	6

Ingredients to be ground (B)

Shallots	360 g, peeled
Garlic	1 whole pod, peeled
Turmeric (*kunyit*)	2.5-cm knob, peeled
Galangal (*lengkuas*)	2.5-cm knob, peeled
Candlenuts (*buah keras*)	3

Method

- Into a bowl, put cucumber and carrot strips. Mix well with 1 Tbsp salt and leave for 30 minutes, then wash thoroughly with water and drain.
- Using a piece of muslin cloth, squeeze out as much water as possible from washed vegetable strips, in small batches.
- To a saucepan half filled with water, add 190 ml vinegar and bring to the boil.
- Lower in all vegetables, including squeezed strips. Then, immediately transfer vegetables to a colander and drain well.
- Put drained vegetables in the sun to dry for 30 minutes.
- Heat oil in a wok. Fry ground ingredients (A) for 2 minutes, then add ground ingredients (B). Fry until fragrant and oil separates.
- Add remaining vinegar, then sugar and 1 tsp salt. Stir in peanuts and mix thoroughly.
- Combine prepared sauce and vegetables and mix well. Keep acar aside for 3 hours before serving.

Otak-Otak Pulau Pinang

Preparation: 25 minutes Cooking: 20 minutes Makes 20 packets

Ingredients

Threadfin (*ikan kurau*)	1 kg, central portion
Salt	as needed
Eggs	6
Kaffir lime leaves (*daun limau purut*)	16, finely sliced
Pure coconut cream (*pati santan*)	315 ml, squeezed from 1 1/2 grated coconuts
Banana leaves	
Pointed pepper leaves (*daun kaduk*)	20
Satay sticks or bamboo skewers	

Ingredients to be ground

Dried chillies	10, soaked
Shallots	8, peeled
Garlic	3 cloves, peeled
Lemon grass (*serai*)	4 stalks
Galangal (*lengkuas*)	4 slices, peeled
Turmeric (*kunyit*)	2.5-cm knob, peeled
Dried prawn (shrimp) paste (*belacan*)	1.25-cm square piece
Candlenuts (*buah keras*)	6
Coriander seeds (*ketumbar biji*)	3 dsp
White peppercorns	36

Method

- Wash and halve fish lengthways, then cut into 5 x 4-cm pieces.
- Season fish pieces with 1 tsp salt and leave for 15 minutes.
- Into a mixing bowl, crack eggs and lightly beat with a fork. Stir in ground ingredients, 3 tsp salt and kaffir lime leaves. Mix with coconut cream.
- Run banana leaves over heat to soften, then cut into 18 x 15-cm pieces; 20 in total. Make sure cut leaves have no holes or slits or gravy will seep through. Wash and dry prepared leaves.
- Onto the centre of each banana leaf, put a pepper leaf and a piece of fish on top. Fold as described in Otak Otak Tenggiri (page 18) and fasten with a *satay* stick. Trim top of excess leaf using scissors.
- Steam parcels for 20 minutes.

Indian Fish Curry

Preparation: 15 minutes Cooking: 20 minutes

Ingredients

Black pomfret (*ikan bawal hitam*)	600 g, cut into 2 portions
Salt	as needed
Cooking oil	100 ml
Fish curry powder	4 Tbsp, mixed with 125 ml water
Mustard seeds	1 tsp
Tamarind pulp (*asam Jawa*)	1 dsp, mixed with 3 Tbsp water and strained
Onion	1, peeled and sliced into rings
Curry leaves	3 sprigs, stems discarded
Coconut cream	250 ml, squeezed from 1 grated coconut with a little water added
Coconut milk	500 ml, squeezed from same grated coconut with sufficient water added
Aubergines (eggplants/ brinjals)	2–3, diagonally sliced
Tomatoes	3, quartered

Ingredients to be ground

Dried chillies	25, soaked
Shallots	240 g, peeled
Lemon grass (*serai*)	4 stalks

Method

- Rub fish with 1 tsp salt and set aside.
- Heat oil in a wok. Fry ground ingredients until fragrant.
- Add curry powder paste and mustard seeds. Fry until fragrant. To prevent mixture from sticking, add a little tamarind juice.
- Add onion rings and curry leaves. Fry for 3 minutes before adding remaining tamarind juice and coconut milk.
- When liquid reaches the boil, add aubergines. Simmer over low heat until soft.
- Add coconut cream and return to the boil. Then, add fish, 1 tsp salt and tomatoes. Simmer until fish is cooked.

Crab Curry

Preparation: 30 minutes Cooking: 25 minutes

Ingredients

Crabs	1.5 kg
Pineapple	1/2, medium, peeled
Cooking oil	5 Tbsp
Shallots	6, peeled and sliced
Garlic	3 cloves, peeled and sliced
Coconut milk	315 ml, squeezed from 1/2 grated coconut with sufficient water added
Salt	1 tsp or to taste

Ingredients to be combined

Ground chillies	1 Tbsp
Ground coriander (*ketumbar serbuk*)	2 Tbsp
Ground turmeric (*kunyit serbuk*)	1 tsp

Ingredients to be ground

Shallots	8, peeled
Garlic	4 cloves, peeled
Ginger	2.5-cm knob, peeled
Cardamoms (*buah pelaga*)	3
Star anise (*bunga lawang*)	2 sections
Cinnamon (*kayu manis*)	1.25-cm stick
Cloves (*bunga cengkih*)	2
Poppy seeds	1 rounded (heaped) tsp
Black peppercorns	1/2 tsp
Skinned coconut	1/2, grated, for *kerisik* (page 11)

Method

- Wash and drain crabs. Dislodge pincers and crack with a pestle. Trim legs and quarter each crab.
- Halve pineapple lengthways, then cut into 2.5-cm thick slices.
- Mix combined ingredients with some water to a paste.
- Heat oil in a wok. Lightly brown shallots and garlic, then add paste and fry for a few minutes. Add ground ingredients and fry until fragrant. Add a little coconut milk to prevent ingredients sticking to wok.
- Add crabs and stir for a few minutes until well coated with ground ingredients. Add remaining coconut milk and bring to the boil.
- Reduce heat. Add pineapple and salt to taste. Simmer for a few minutes or until crabs are cooked and very little gravy remains.

Kurma

Preparation: 20 minutes Cooking: (Beef) 45–60 minutes, (Chicken) 30 minutes

Ingredients

Beef	1 kg, or 1 chicken, about 1.5 kg
Ghee (clarified butter)	3 Tbsp
Shallots	10, peeled and sliced
Garlic	3 cloves, peeled and sliced
Cinnamon (*kayu manis*)	2.5-cm stick
Cardamoms (*buah pelaga*)	4
Kurma curry powder	4 Tbsp, mixed with a little water into a paste
Salt	1 1/2 tsp
Coconut milk	750 ml, squeezed from 1 grated coconut with sufficient water added
Powdered milk	2 rounded (heaped) Tbsp, mixed with 125 ml water
Lime (*limau nipis*) juice	squeezed from 1 lime
Onions	2, peeled and prepared as described on page 132
Mint leaves	4 sprigs

Method

- Cut beef into small pieces. If using chicken, cut into bite-size pieces.
- In an earthen pot, heat ghee and fry shallots, garlic, cinnamon and cardamoms until fragrant.
- Add curry paste and fry over low heat until fragrant.
- Add meat and salt. Cook over low heat until meat is almost tender, adding a little coconut milk to prevent meat from sticking to pot.
- Pour in remaining coconut milk and bring to the boil. Then, combine powdered milk mixture and lime juice and add to pot.
- When liquid returns to the boil, add onions and simmer over low heat for 20 minutes or until meat is tender and oil separates.
- Add mint leaves just before removing from heat.

Udang Tumis Petai

Preparation: 30 minutes Cooking: 15 minutes

Ingredients

Stink beans (*petai*)	15 pods
Cooking oil	4 Tbsp
Prawns (shrimps)	600 g, small, peeled
Tamarind pulp (*asam Jawa*)	1 rounded (heaped) Tbsp, mixed with 125 ml water and strained
Sugar	1 tsp
Salt	1 1/2 tsp

Ingredients to be ground (A)

Galangal (*lengkuas*)	2.5-cm knob, peeled
Turmeric (*kunyit*)	2.5-cm knob, peeled
Cashew nuts	10, roasted
Lemon grass (*serai*)	4 stalks

Ingredients to be ground (B)

Dried chillies	20, soaked
Red chillies	5
Bird's eye chillies (*cili padi*)	5
Shallots	240 g, peeled
Garlic	2 cloves, peeled
Dried prawn (shrimp) paste (*belacan*)	4 x 2.5-cm piece

Method

- Remove stink beans from pods and peel off outer skins.
- Heat oil in a wok and fry ground ingredients (A) until fragrant.
- Add ground ingredients (B) and fry over low heat until fragrant and oil separates.
- Add prawns and stir-fry for a few minutes, taking care not to overcook them.
- Pour in tamarind juice and bring to a slow boil.
- Add stink beans, sugar and salt. Stir-fry for 2 minutes and dish out.

Kari Kambing

Preparation: 20 minutes Cooking: 30 minutes

Ingredients

Mutton	600 g
Cooking oil	4 Tbsp
Curry leaves	1 sprig, stem discarded
Coconut cream	250 ml, squeezed from 1/2 grated coconut
Coconut milk	375 ml, squeezed from same grated coconut with sufficient water added
Meat curry powder	2 Tbsp
Ground fennel (*jintan manis serbuk*)	1/2 Tbsp
Potatoes	3, peeled, quartered and fried
Lime (*limau nipis*) juice	squeezed from 1/2 lime
Salt	2 tsp

Ingredients to be sliced

Shallots	12, peeled
Garlic	5 cloves, peeled
Ginger	4-cm knob, peeled

Spices

Cinnamon (*kayu manis*)	5-cm stick
Star anise (*bunga lawang*)	1 whole
Cardamoms (*buah pelaga*)	2
Cloves (*bunga cengkih*)	4

Method

- Cut mutton into 2.5-cm cubes. Set aside.
- In a pressure cooker, heat oil and brown sliced ingredients and curry leaves. Then, add spices and fry until fragrant.
- Add mutton cubes and fry for a few minutes, then add coconut milk. Cover and pressure cook for 10 minutes.
- At the end of that time, release pressure and uncover to add coconut cream.
- When liquid reaches the boil, stir in curry powder and fennel. If a thicker curry is preferred, simmer over low heat for 5 minutes more before adding potatoes and simmer until cooked.
- Stir in lime juice and salt before removing from heat.

Rendang Daging

Preparation: 20 minutes Cooking: 1 hour 30 minutes

Ingredients

Beef	1 kg
Cooking oil	125 ml
Shallots	300 g, peeled and coarsely ground
Lemon grass (*serai*)	2 stalks, lightly crushed
Meat curry powder	2 Tbsp
Pure coconut cream (*pati santan*)	125 ml, squeezed from 1 grated coconut
Coconut milk	625 ml, squeezed from same grated coconut with sufficient water added
Salt	2 rounded (heaped) tsp or to taste

Ingredients to be ground

Dried chillies	40, soaked and seeded
Red chillies	5, seeded
Garlic	4 cloves, peeled
Ginger	2.5-cm knob, peeled
Turmeric (*kunyit*)	4-cm knob, peeled
Lemon grass (*serai*)	2 stalks
Cashew nuts	10, untoasted

Method

- Cut meat across grain and into thin 4-cm slices. Set aside.
- Heat oil in a wok. Fry shallots for 5 minutes or until lightly browned.
- Add ground ingredients and lemon grass. Fry over low heat until fragrant.
- Mix curry powder with a little coconut milk, then add to wok and continue frying until oil separates. If necessary, add more coconut milk to prevent mixture from sticking to wok.
- Add beef and fry until water from meat evaporates, then pour in remaining coconut milk. Simmer until thick, stirring occasionally.
- Add coconut cream and salt to taste. Continue cooking, stirring all the time, to prevent ingredients from sticking, until gravy is thick and meat tender.
- Serve with rice.

Ayam Tumis

Preparation: 25 minutes Cooking: 30 minutes

Ingredients

Chicken	1, about 1.5 kg
Cooking oil	100 ml
Torch ginger buds (*bunga kantan*)	2, finely sliced
Lemon grass (*serai*)	2 stalks, crushed
Tamarind pulp (*asam Jawa*)	2 Tbsp, mixed with 750 ml water and strained
Sugar	1 Tbsp
Salt	2 tsp

Ingredients to be ground

Dried chillies	35–40, soaked
Dried prawn (shrimp) paste (*belacan*)	5 x 2.5-cm piece
Lemon grass (*serai*)	4 stalks
Garlic	6 cloves, peeled
Galangal (*lengkuas*)	10 slices, peeled
Turmeric (*kunyit*)	4-cm knob, peeled
Shallots	240 g, peeled

Method

- Cut chicken into serving-size pieces. Set aside.
- Heat oil in a wok. Fry torch ginger buds and lemon grass for 1–2 minutes, then add ground ingredients and fry until fragrant.
- Add chicken pieces and stir-fry until well coated with ground ingredients. Then, add tamarind juice and bring to the boil.
- Add all remaining ingredients, reduce heat and allow to simmer for 15–20 minutes or until chicken is tender.
- Serve with rice.

Kari Ayam Kering

Preparation: 20 minutes Cooking: 35 minutes

Ingredients

Chicken	1, about 1 kg, cut into bite-size pieces
Salt	as needed
Meat curry powder	2 Tbsp
Cooking oil	4 Tbsp
Onions	2, peeled and sliced
Potatoes	3, peeled, quartered and soaked in salted water
Coconut cream	250 ml, squeezed from 1 grated coconut with a little water added
Coconut milk	375 ml, squeezed from same grated coconut with sufficient water added
Curry leaves	2 sprigs, stems discarded

Ingredients to be ground

Red chillies	8
Shallots	8, peeled
Garlic	2 cloves, peeled
Ginger	3 slices, peeled
Cloves (*bunga cengkih*)	3
Cardamoms (*buah pelaga*)	8

Method

- Season chicken with 1 tsp salt, curry powder and ground ingredients. Leave for 30 minutes.
- Heat oil in a wok and fry onion slices until transparent and fragrant. Drain from oil and set aside.
- In the same oil, fry drained potatoes for 5 minutes until lightly browned. Drain and set aside.
- To wok, add seasoned chicken and fry for 10 minutes, then add coconut milk and curry leaves. Bring to the boil, then simmer gently until chicken is almost tender.
- Add fried potatoes, 1 tsp salt and coconut cream. Cook over low heat, stirring frequently, until chicken is tender and gravy dry.
- Serve garnished with fried onion slices.

Encik Kebin

Preparation: 10 minutes   Cooking: 10 minutes

Ingredients

Chicken	1, about 1.5 kg, cut into 5-cm pieces
Ginger juice	1 tsp
Salt	1 1/2 tsp
Pure coconut cream (*pati santan*)	125 ml, squeezed from 1/2 grated coconut
Cooking oil for deep-frying	

Ingredients to be ground

Dried chillies	15, soaked
Coriander seeds (*ketumbar biji*)	1 Tbsp
Fennel seeds (*jintan manis biji*)	2 tsp
Cumin seeds (*jintan putih biji*)	1 tsp
Cinnamon (*kayu manis*)	1.25-cm stick
Cloves (*bunga cengkih*)	2
Ground white pepper	1 tsp
Ground turmeric (*kunyit serbuk*)	1/2 tsp

Garnishing

Cucumber slices

Tomato slices

Method

- Wash chicken pieces and pat dry.
- Into a mixing bowl, put chicken, ground ingredients, ginger juice, salt and coconut cream. Mix well and leave to marinate for at least 1 hour.
- Heat oil for deep-frying in a wok until smoking hot. Lower in chicken pieces and deep-fry without stirring for 2 minutes.
- Reduce heat and continue cooking until golden brown. When done, remove to a garnished serving plate.

Penang Rojak

Preparation: 20 minutes Cooking: 10 minutes

Ingredients

Cucumber	1
Green mangoes	2, small, peeled
Pineapple	$^1/_2$, medium, peeled
Yam bean (*bangkuang*)	300 g, peeled
Rojak Sauce*	1 recipe
Black prawn (shrimp) paste (*hae ko*)	3 tsp
Peanut candy or roasted peanuts	150 g, coarsely ground
Sesame seeds	1 Tbsp, roasted

Method

- Cut cucumber, mangoes, pineapple and yam bean into small wedges and combine in a large mixing bowl.
- Add cooled *rojak* sauce and prawn paste. Mix well.
- Add peanut candy or roasted peanuts and sesame seeds. Stir well and serve immediately.

Rojak* Sauce

Tamarind pulp (*asam Jawa*)	4 rounded (heaped) Tbsp, mixed with 125 ml water and strained
Sugar	5 Tbsp
Dark soy sauce	1 tsp

Ingredients to be ground

Dried chillies	25, soaked
Dried prawn (shrimp) paste (*belacan*)	2.5-cm square piece

Method

- Into a small saucepan, put ground ingredients and tamarind juice. Cook over low heat.
- Stir in sugar and dark soy sauce and continue cooking until sugar dissolves and sauce is thick. Allow to cool.

Nasi Kunyit

Preparation: 15 minutes Cooking: 1 hour 15 minutes

Ingredients

Glutinous rice	1.25 kg
Dried turmeric (*kunyit kering*)	4 large pieces
Salt	1 tsp
Banana leaves	
Pure coconut cream (*pati santan*)	500 ml, squeezed from $2^1/_2$ grated coconuts
Salt	$^1/_2$ tsp

Method

- Wash and drain rice. Then, crush turmeric pieces and wrap with a piece of clean cloth. Soak rice in water overnight with wrapped turmeric and 1 tsp salt added.
- On cooking day, line base of a shallow bamboo basket with banana leaves, then put rice on top.
- Prepare steamer for use. When water is boiling rapidly, put in basket and steam for 1 hour or until rice is cooked and soft.
- Transfer cooked rice to a heatproof dish or pot. Pour in coconut cream mixed with $^1/_2$ tsp salt, stirring well with a spoon at the same time.
- Return rice to steamer and steam for 10–15 minutes more. When done, transfer rice to a serving plate and lightly press into a mound with a spoon.
- Serve with any chicken curry.

Penang Laksa

Preparation: 1 hour 30 minutes Cooking: 30 minutes

Ingredients

Tamarind pulp (*asam Jawa*)	4 Tbsp, mixed with 250 ml water and strained
Water	1.5 litres
Polygonum leaves (*daun kesum*)	10–12 sprigs, discard stems
Torch ginger buds (*bunga kantan*)	3–4, buds split and stems smashed
Dried sour fruit (*asam gelugur*)	4 slices
Wolf herring (*ikan parang*)	1.75 kg, steamed and flaked
Sugar	2 Tbsp
Salt	to taste
Fresh round rice noodles (*laksa*)	600 g, parboiled

Ingredients to be ground

Dried chillies	40, soaked
Galangal (*lengkuas*)	6 slices, peeled
Dried prawn (shrimp) paste (*belacan*)	5 x 2.5 x 1.25-cm piece
Lemon grass (*serai*)	3 stalks
Shallots	180 g, peeled

Garnishing

Pineapple	1/2, peeled, cut into strips
Cucumber	1, peeled and shredded
Lettuce	1/2 head, finely shredded
Onion	1, peeled and finely sliced
Red chillies	3, seeded and sliced
Mint leaves	1 sprig, stem discarded
Kalamansi limes (*limau kesturi*)	6–8, halved
Black prawn (shrimp) paste (*hae ko*)	as needed, diluted with a little water

Method

- In an earthen pot, bring tamarind juice, ground ingredients and water to boil. Add polygonum leaves, torch ginger buds and dried sour fruit. Simmer over low heat for 15 minutes. Add flaked fish, sugar and salt to taste. Continue to simmer.
- Remove polygonum leaves, torch ginger buds and dried sour fruit slices before dishing out gravy.
- To serve, dish noodles into individual serving bowls and top with garnishing. Ladle hot gravy over and drizzle with 1 tsp diluted prawn paste. Serve immediately.

Kuih Ko Swee

Preparation: 15 minutes Cooking: 25 minutes

Ingredients

Palm sugar (*gula Melaka*)	180 g, chopped
Sugar	60 g
Water	250 ml
Screwpine (*pandan*) leaves	2, washed and knotted
Chinese teacups	22, small
Grated skinned young coconut	150 g
Salt	a pinch

Combination (A)

Wet rice flour	150 g
Sago flour	120 g
Water	250 ml
Slaked lime	1/8 tsp
Alkaline water (*kan sui*)	1 tsp

Combination (B)

Dry rice flour	150 g
Sago flour	60 g
Water	375 ml
Borax (*pangsar*)	1/8 tsp
Alkaline water (*kan sui*)	1 tsp

Method

- In a saucepan, put both sugars, water and screwpine leaves. Bring to a slow boil, cooking until sugars dissolve.
- Use either combination (A) or (B). If using (A), blend all ingredients in a bowl until smooth. Strain hot, boiled syrup gradually into flour mixture, stirring until well mixed.
- If using (B), sift rice and sago flours in a mixing bowl, then add water and mix until smooth. Strain cooked syrup gradually into flour mixture, stirring until well mixed, then stir in borax and alkaline water.
- Prepare steamer for use. When water is boiling rapidly, put in Chinese teacups and steam for 5 minutes.
- Stir flour mixture thoroughly, then fill cups. For easier filling, transfer mixture to a large measuring jug. There should be approximately 3 cups of flour mixture.
- Steam filled cups over moderate heat for 20 minutes. Remove and leave to cool.
- Remove cooled *kuih* from cups and roll in grated coconut mixed with salt.

Roti Jala (Lacy Pancake)

Preparation: 15 minutes   Cooking: 30 minutes   Makes 24

Ingredients

Plain (all-purpose) flour	240 g
Salt	1/2 tsp
Eggs	2, beaten
Coconut milk	625 ml, squeezed from 1/2 grated skinned coconut with sufficient water added

Roti jala cup

Method

- Sift flour into a bowl and add salt. Stir in beaten eggs and coconut milk, then beat until smooth. Strain batter if it is lumpy.
- Grease and heat a non-stick pan over low heat.
- Put a ladleful of batter into *roti jala* cup and move it in a circular motion over pan so that pancake will have a lacy pattern.
- Cook pancake until set, then turn over onto a dish. Repeat making pancakes until batter is used up.
- When cool, fold pancakes in half twice or fold once and roll up. Serve with curry kapitan (page 218) or your favourite curry.

Note: A special cup which has 4–5 funnels extending from its base is required for making *roti jala*.

Chicken Biryani

Preparation: 20 minutes Cooking: 40 minutes

Ingredients

Ghee (clarified butter)	3 Tbsp
Cinnamon (*kayu manis*)	2 sticks, each 9-cm long
Star anise (*bunga lawang*)	3 whole
Onions	5, peeled and sliced
Chicken	1, about 1.5 kg, cut into 6 large pieces
Ground turmeric (*kunyit serbuk*)	1 dsp
Yoghurt	1/2 cup
Tomatoes	4, quartered
Green chillies	4, kept whole
Salt	1 Tbsp
Curry leaves	3 sprigs, stems discarded
Coconut milk	875 ml, squeezed from 1/2 grated coconut with sufficient water added
Ground almonds	1 Tbsp
Ground cashew nuts	1 Tbsp
Basmati (long grain) rice	480 g, washed and drained
Screwpine (*pandan*) leaves	3, washed and knotted

Ingredients to be ground

Ginger	1.25-cm knob, peeled
Garlic	3 cloves, peeled
Shallots	8, peeled
Chilli powder	1 tsp
Black peppercorns	1 tsp

Method

- In a pan, heat ghee and fry cinnamon and star anise for 1 minute, then lightly brown onions.
- Add chicken and fry well, then add turmeric and ground ingredients.
- Add yoghurt, tomatoes, green chillies, salt and curry leaves. Simmer gently for a few minutes.
- Pour in half the coconut milk and stir in ground almonds and cashew nuts.
- Bring to the boil, then add remaining coconut milk.
- Put well drained rice and chicken curry mixture into a pot or rice cooker to finish cooking. Halfway through cooking, add screwpine leaves and stir well.
- Discard screwpine leaves before serving.
- Serve hot, each serving with a portion of chicken.

Curry Kapitan

Preparation: 20 minutes   Cooking: 40 minutes

Ingredients

Chicken	1, about 1.5 kg
Cooking oil	3 Tbsp
Onions	2, peeled and diced
Salt	2 tsp
Coconut cream	250 ml, squeezed from 1 grated coconut with a little water added
Coconut milk	750 ml, squeezed from same grated coconut with sufficient water added
Limes (*limau nipis*) juice	squeezed from 1–2 limes

Ingredients to be ground

Red chillies	15
Shallots	15, peeled
Garlic	4 cloves, peeled
Turmeric (*kunyit*)	2.5-cm knob, peeled
Candlenuts (*buah keras*)	10
Dried prawn (shrimp) paste (*belacan*)	5 x 2.5-cm piece
Lemon grass (*serai*)	4 stalks

Method

- Cut chicken into bite-size pieces. Set aside.
- Heat oil in a wok and lightly brown onions with salt.
- Add ground ingredients and fry until fragrant, adding a little coconut cream to prevent ingredients from sticking to wok, if necessary.
- Add chicken pieces and fry for a few minutes, then pour in coconut milk and cook over low heat until chicken is tender.
- Add remaining coconut cream. When liquid returns to the boil, add lime juice.
- Serve curry kapitan with rice or roti jala (page 214).

Dalca

Preparation: 25 minutes   Cooking: 1 hour 15 minutes

Ingredients

Beef	600 g, with bones
Meat curry powder	3 rounded (heaped) Tbsp
Salt	2 tsp
Coconut cream	250 ml, squeezed from 1 grated coconut with a little water added
Coconut milk	750 ml, squeezed from same grated coconut with sufficient water added
Potatoes	300 g, peeled and cut into wedges
Aubergines (eggplants/brinjals)	3, cut into 1.25-cm wide slices
Tamarind pulp (*asam Jawa*)	2 Tbsp, mixed with 5 Tbsp water and strained
Lentils	1/2 cup
Tomatoes	3, quartered
Green chillies	4
Cooking oil	2 Tbsp
Shallots	6, peeled and sliced
Ginger	2.5-cm knob, peeled and sliced

Spices

Cinnamon (*kayu manis*)	2.5-cm stick
Cardamoms (*buah pelaga*)	3
Star anise (*bunga lawang*)	2 sections

Method

- Cut beef into 4-cm cubes. Set aside.
- Into an earthen pot, put beef cubes, curry powder, spices, salt and coconut milk.
- Bring to a slow boil.
- Reduce heat and simmer for 40 minutes or until beef is tender.
- Add potatoes and simmer for 10 minutes more, then add aubergines and simmer until almost soft.
- Add coconut cream, tamarind juice and lentils.
- When liquid reaches the boil, add tomatoes and green chillies. Cook for 3 minutes, then remove from heat.
- Heat 2 Tbsp oil in a wok. Brown shallots and ginger. Pour over Dalca and stir to mix well.
- Serve with rice or *roti canai*, a type of flat bread.

Ayam Masak Cabai

Preparation: 20 minutes   Cooking 35 minutes

Ingredients

Chicken	1, about 1.5 kg, cut into serving-size pieces
Dried sour fruit (*asam gelugur*)	2 pieces
Coconut milk	750 ml, squeezed from 1 grated coconut with sufficient water added
Condensed tomato soup	1/2 can (285 g)
Tomatoes	3, quartered
Salt	1 1/2 tsp
Mint leaves	4 sprigs

Ingredients to be ground

Red chillies	300 g, seeded
Ginger	2.5-cm knob, peeled
Onions	2, peeled

Method

- Into an earthen pot, put chicken, ground ingredients, dried sour fruit slices, coconut milk and tomato soup. Bring to a slow boil.
- Reduce heat and simmer over low heat for 30 minutes, stirring frequently, until chicken is tender and oil separates.
- Add tomatoes and salt. Cook for 2 minutes more.
- Just before removing from heat, throw in mint leaves.

Kedah

Kedah, rice bowl of Malaysia, is situated in the north of Peninsular Malaysia. As far as the eye can see are stretches of flat *padi* fields and in the harvesting season, the rich golden fields are a bustle of activity.

Malay cuisine is a delicious reflection of cooking styles in the north. Laksa Kedah, tangy sour with flaked fish, is good and *pedas* (spicy). Dalca Daging Kedah is a vegetable curry given added flavour with beef bones. The Arabian influence in Acar Limau and Masak Arab Daging makes them deliciously different.

Masak Arab Daging

Preparation: 20 minutes Cooking: 1 hour

Ingredients

Beef	1 kg, cut into thin 5-cm slices
Cooking oil	3 Tbsp
Shallots	6, peeled and sliced
Garlic	4 cloves, peeled and sliced
Coconut milk	1 litre, squeezed from 1 grated coconut with sufficient water added
Tomato purée	1 small can (70 g)
Salt	1 1/2 tsp or to taste

Ingredients to be ground

Ripe tomatoes	300 g
Shallots	300 g, peeled
Sesame seeds	90 g
Fennel seeds (*jintan manis biji*)	1/2 tsp
Cumin seeds (*jintan putih biji*)	1/2 tsp
Ground white pepper	1/2 tsp
Ginger	1.25-cm knob, peeled
Turmeric (*kunyit*)	2.5-cm knob, peeled

Method

- Mix beef slices with ground ingredients and leave for 1 hour.
- Heat oil in a wok. Brown shallots and garlic.
- Add meat and fry gently until water evaporates.
- Add coconut milk and stir until liquid reaches the boil.
- Reduce heat and simmer gently, stirring frequently, until gravy is thick and meat tender.
- Add tomato purée and simmer for 5 minutes, stirring continuously. Add salt to taste.

Opor Ayam

Preparation: 15 minutes Cooking: 30 minutes

Ingredients

Cooking oil	3 Tbsp
Chicken	1, about 1.5 kg, cut into bite-size pieces
Coconut milk	750 ml, squeezed from 1 grated coconut with sufficient water added
Salt	2 tsp or to taste

Ingredients to be ground

Shallots	12, peeled
Garlic	4 cloves, peeled
Ginger	2.5-cm knob, peeled
Galangal (*lengkuas*)	2.5-cm knob, peeled
Lemon grass (*serai*)	2 stalks
Coriander seeds (*ketumbar biji*)	1 Tbsp
White peppercorns	1 tsp
Candlenuts (*buah keras*)	10

Method

- Heat oil in a wok. Fry ground ingredients over low heat until fragrant and oil separates.
- Add chicken and fry well for 3 minutes, then pour in coconut milk. Bring to a slow boil.
- Reduce heat and simmer for 20 minutes or until chicken is tender. Add salt to taste.
- Serve opor ayam with white rice.

Note: Three *salam* leaves (*daun salam*) may be added, if available, to give fragrance.

Ketupat Pulut

Preparation: 30 minutes Cooking: 2 hours 30 minutes

Ingredients

Coconut cream	875 ml, squeezed from 3 grated coconuts with a little water added
Salt	1½ tsp
Glutinous rice	1 kg, washed and drained
Banana leaves	10 pieces, each trimmed to 23 x 18 cm and scalded

Method

- In a large saucepan, combine coconut cream and salt. Bring to a slow boil over low heat.
- Add glutinous rice and stir for 10–15 minutes or until almost dry.
- Cover saucepan and cook over low heat for 20 minutes or until glutinous rice is half-cooked. Remove from heat.
- Onto the centre of each banana leaf, put 3–4 Tbsp cooled, half-cooked glutinous rice, then roll into a long roll about 4 cm in diameter.
- Twist and tie the 2 ends of each roll securely with strong string or triple strength nylon threads. Secure roll by tying string around the centre as well.
- Prepare a steamer for use. When ready, steam glutinous rice rolls for 2 hours over low heat.
- Remove rolls from steamer and leave to cool. Discard banana leaves and cut rolls into 2.5-cm thick slices. Serve with serunding daging, Kedah style (page 230).

Mee Kedah

Preparation: 25 minutes Cooking: 30 minutes

Ingredients

Fresh yellow (Hokkien) noodles	600 g
Cooking oil	5 Tbsp
Beef	300 g, cut into thin strips
Water	1.5 litres
Dried prawns (shrimps) (*hae be*)	120 g, ground
Prawns (shrimps)	300 g, small, peeled
Condensed tomato soup	1/2 can (285 g)
Salt	to taste
Chinese flowering cabbage (*chye sim*)	300 g, cut into 5-cm lengths, stems and leaves separated

Ingredients to be ground

Dried chillies	20, soaked
Shallots	8, peeled
Garlic	3 cloves, peeled

Garnishing

Hard-boiled eggs	4, shelled
Firm bean curd (*tau kwa*)	2 pieces, fried and cut into thick slices
Bean sprouts	300 g, tailed
Tomatoes	2, sliced
Red chillies	5, sliced
Crisp-fried shallots	
Chopped spring onions (scallions)	
Chopped Chinese celery	

Method

- Scald noodles in boiling water, drain and mix with 1 Tbsp oil to prevent noodles from sticking. Transfer to a large serving dish.
- Into a pot, put beef and add 1.5 litres water. Bring to the boil and cook until beef is tender.
- In a clean pot, heat 4 Tbsp oil and fry ground ingredients for a few minutes. Add dried prawns and fry until fragrant and crisp.
- Add beef and stock from first pot and bring to the boil.
- Add prawns, tomato soup and salt to taste.
- Put in vegetable stems, then leaves. When cooked, pour over noodles. Garnish as desired and serve.

Panggang Ikan Terubuk

Preparation: 10 minutes Grilling: 15 minutes

Ingredients

Hilsa or shad (*ikan terubuk*)	1, medium, cleaned but with scales left on

Ingredients to be ground

Red chillies	2
Bird's eye chillies (*cili padi*)	6
Lemon grass (*serai*)	1 stalk
Shallots	6, peeled
Turmeric (*kunyit*)	2.5-cm knob, peeled
Grated coconut	1 Tbsp
Salt	2 tsp

Method

- Rub fish all over with ground ingredients and leave for 30 minutes.
- Grill over glowing charcoal on both sides for about 15 minutes or until cooked.
- Remove scales and serve hot with white rice.

Serunding Daging, Kedah Style

Preparation: 30 minutes   Cooking: 2 hours

Ingredients

Beef	300 g
Kaffir lime leaves (*daun limau purut*)	2, finely sliced
Turmeric leaf (*daun kunyit*)	1, finely sliced
Tamarind pulp (*asam Jawa*)	1 rounded (heaped) tsp, mixed with 3 Tbsp water and strained
Sugar	1 Tbsp
Coconut milk	250 ml, squeezed from 1/2 grated coconut with sufficient water added
Skinned coconut	1/2, grated, dry-roasted until light brown
Salt	1 1/2 tsp

Ingredients to be ground

Dried chillies	15, soaked
Shallots	10, peeled
Garlic	2 cloves, peeled
Lemon grass (*serai*)	2 stalks
Galangal (*lengkuas*)	2.5-cm knob, peeled
Ginger	1.25-cm knob, peeled
Dried prawn (shrimp) paste (*belacan*)	2.5-cm square piece
Coriander seeds (*ketumbar biji*)	2 Tbsp
Cumin seeds (*jintan putih biji*)	1 tsp

Method

- In a saucepan, simmer beef with enough water to cover meat for 1 hour. Alternatively, pressure cook for 30 minutes.
- Remove cooked beef and drain in a colander until dry and cool.
- Cut cooled meat into 2.5-cm cubes, then shred finely with fingers.
- Mix meat shreds with ground ingredients, kaffir lime and turmeric leaves, tamarind juice and sugar. Leave for 15 minutes.
- Into a wok, put marinated meat and coconut milk. Bring to a slow boil.
- Reduce heat and fry continuously until almost dry, then add grated coconut and salt to taste.
- Cook over very low heat for 30 minutes more, stirring all the time, or until completely dry.

Dalca Daging Kedah

Preparation: 25 minutes   Cooking: 35 minutes

Ingredients

Beef	300 g, with or without bones, cut into 2.5-cm pieces
Skinned coconut	1/2, grated, for *kerisik* (page 11)
Cooking oil	3 Tbsp
Coconut milk	750 ml, squeezed from 1/2 grated coconut with sufficient water added
Aubergine (eggplant/brinjal)	1, diagonally cut into 2.5-cm slices
Long (snake) beans	5, cut into 5-cm lengths
Red chillies	2, seeded and split
Blimbing (*belimbing*)	4, halved lengthwise
Potatoes	2, cut into 2-cm cubes and fried
Tomatoes	2, quartered
Salt	2 tsp or to taste

Ingredients to be ground

Dried chillies	15, soaked
Coriander seeds (*ketumbar biji*)	2 tsp
Fennel seeds (*jintan manis biji*)	1/2 tsp
Cumin seeds (*jintan putih biji*)	1/2 tsp
Cinnamon (*kayu manis*)	0.6-cm stick
Clove (*bunga cengkih*)	1
Star anise (*bunga lawang*)	1 section
Black peppercorns	1/2 tsp
Ground turmeric (*kunyit serbuk*)	1/2 tsp

Method

- Mix beef with *kerisik* and leave for 15 minutes.
- Heat oil in a pot and fry ground ingredients until fragrant and oil separates.
- Add meat and fry for 5 minutes, then add coconut milk and bring to the boil.
- Add aubergine, long beans, chillies, blimbing, and potatoes. Simmer over low heat until vegetables are tender.
- Put in tomatoes and add salt to taste.

Masak Asam Ikan Kerapu

Preparation: 10 minutes   Cooking: 15 minutes

Ingredients

Garoupa (*ikan kerapu*)	3 slices, or black pomfret (*ikan bawal hitam*)
Salt	1 tsp
Turmeric (*kunyit*)	2.5-cm knob, peeled and ground
Cooking oil	2 Tbsp
Coconut milk	375 ml, squeezed from 1/2 grated coconut with sufficient water added
Red chillies	3, seeded and sliced
Ginger	2 slices, peeled and cut into strips
Shallots	3, peeled and sliced
Garlic	3 cloves, peeled and sliced
Dried sour fruit (*asam gelugur*)	2 pieces
Salt	1/2 tsp

Method

- Season fish with 1 tsp salt and turmeric. Set aside.
- Heat oil in a wok until hot. Fry fish for 2 minutes on each side. Dish out.
- Into a pot, put all remaining ingredients. Bring to a slow boil, then simmer for 5 minutes over low heat.
- Add fried fish slices and leave to boil for 2 minutes.

Laksa Kedah

Preparation: 1 hour   Cooking: 30–35 minutes   Serves approximately 10

Ingredients

Fresh thick round rice (*laksa*) noodles	600 g
Mackerel	1.25 kg
Water	3 litres
Dried sour fruit (*asam gelugur*)	6 pieces
Torch ginger buds (*bunga kantan*)	3 stalks, buds split and stems lightly crushed
Polygonum leaves (*daun kesum*)	2 small bunches
Mint leaves	a few sprigs
Prawns (shrimps)	450 g, small and peeled
Salt	to taste

Ingredients to be ground

Dried chillies	40, soaked
Shallots	25, peeled
Dried prawn (shrimp) paste (*belacan*)	5 x 1-cm piece

Garnishing

Hard-boiled eggs	6, shelled
Onions	2, peeled and finely sliced
Cucumber	1, shredded
Lettuce	1/2 head, shredded
Red chillies	5, sliced
Mint leaves	

Method

- Scald noodles in boiling water for 3–4 minutes and drain well.
- Steam fish for 12 minutes, then extract flesh. Reserve bones separately.
- Blend fish bones with 750 ml water. Pour into a saucepan and bring to a slow boil, then simmer for 10 minutes. Strain stock into an earthen pot.
- Blend fish meat with a little water. Transfer to earthen pot and add remaining water.
- Add ground ingredients, dried sour fruit and torch ginger buds, as well as polygonum and mint leaves. Bring to a slow boil.
- Simmer gently for 20–25 minutes before adding prawns and salt to taste.
- To serve, put some noodles into individual serving bowls. Top with a little of each garnishing ingredient and ladle gravy over. Serve hot.

Acar Limau

Preparation: 20 minutes Cooking: 25 minutes

Ingredients

Cooking oil	8 Tbsp
Dried chillies	100 g, soaked and ground
Vinegar	190 ml
Water	750 ml
Sugar	6 Tbsp
Salt	2 Tbsp
Pickled kalamansi limes (*limau kesturi*)	100 g
Shallots	150 g, peeled and kept whole
Garlic	100 g, peeled and kept whole
Ginger	7.5-cm knob, peeled and shredded
Preserved radish (*chye poh*)	100 g, cut into 1.25-cm cubes
Dried blimbing (*belimbing kering*)	60 g
Prunes	100 g
Dried Chinese red dates (*hung cho*)	100 g
Red chillies	4, split lengthwise without cutting through
Green chillies	4, split lengthwise without cutting through
Mustard seeds	2 Tbsp, roasted
Sesame seeds	2 Tbsp, roasted

Ingredients to be ground

Shallots	5, peeled
Garlic	4 cloves, peeled
Cloves (*bunga cengkih*)	7
Star anise (*bunga lawang*)	2 sections
Cinnamon (*kayu manis*)	5-cm stick

Method

- Heat oil in a wok. Fry ground ingredients until fragrant, then add ground dried chillies and fry until oil separates.
- Add vinegar, water, sugar and salt. Bring to a slow boil, then simmer over low heat for 10 minutes or until slightly thickened.
- Except mustard and sesame seeds, add all other ingredients. Mix well and simmer over low heat for 10 minutes more.
- Just before removing from heat, add mustard and sesame seeds.

Note: To pickle kalamansi limes, boil 375 ml vinegar with 240 g sugar and 2 Tbsp salt. Put in limes and when cooled, keep in airtight jars for at least 2 weeks before using.

Kanji Kedah (Kedah Porridge)

Preparation: 15 minutes   Cooking: 1 hour

Ingredients

Rice	480 g
Water	2 litres
Beef or chicken	240 g, cut into thin strips
Prawns (shrimps)	240 g, small, peeled
Ginger	2.5-cm knob, peeled and shredded
Lemon grass (*serai*)	1 stalk, lightly crushed
Fenugreek seeds (*halba*)	1 tsp
Salt	to taste
Coconut milk	190 ml, squeezed from 1/2 grated coconut with sufficient water added

Garnishing

Crisp-fried shallots

Chopped spring onions (scallions)

Sliced lettuce leaves

Method

- Boil rice with 2 litres water over low heat for 40 minutes or until grains are broken and porridge has a thick consistency.
- Add beef or chicken, prawns, ginger, lemon grass and fenugreek. Bring to a slow boil and add salt to taste.
- When porridge returns to the boil, stir in coconut milk and remove from heat.
- Garnish and serve hot.

Perlis

Perlis, the smallest state in Peninsular Malaysia, abuts the Thai border. The state capital of Kangar is surrounded by limestone hills.

In this region, curry dishes cooked with lots of coconut milk — like Gulai Daging and Kurma Daging Perlis — are all-time favourites. The people make tasty use of local ingredients and their dishes, though spicy, are delectable and simple to prepare.

Kurma Daging Perlis

Preparation: 20 minutes Cooking: 45 minutes

Ingredients

Beef	600 g
Kurma curry powder	3 Tbsp
Cooking oil	125 ml
Coconut cream	250 ml, squeezed from 1 grated coconut with a little water added
Coconut milk	1 litre, squeezed from same grated coconut with sufficient water added
Dried sour fruit (*asam gelugur*)	1 large piece
Onions	2, peeled and quartered
Salt	1 1/2 tsp

Ingredients to be ground

Shallots	10, peeled
Garlic	5 cloves, peeled
Galangal (*lengkuas*)	2.5-cm knob, peeled
Ginger	2.5-cm knob, peeled
Turmeric (*kunyit*)	1.25-cm knob, peeled
Lemon grass (*serai*)	3 stalks, sliced
Black peppercorns	1 tsp
Freshly grated skinned coconut	4 Tbsp

Ingredients to be sliced

Shallots	4, peeled
Garlic	2 cloves, peeled
Ginger	2.5-cm knob, peeled

Spices

Star anise (*bunga lawang*)	3 sections
Cloves (*bunga cengkih*)	3
Cinnamon (*kayu manis*)	1.25-cm stick

Method

- Slice beef thinly and across grain.
- Into a mixing bowl, put beef, *kurma* curry powder and ground ingredients. Mix well and leave for 15 minutes.
- Heat oil in a wok. Fry sliced ingredients and spices until fragrant.
- Add beef and fry for a few minutes, then pour in coconut milk. Add dried sour fruit and bring to a slow boil.
- Reduce heat and simmer until meat is almost tender.
- Add onions, salt and coconut cream. Simmer for 5 minutes more.

Note: For *kenduris*, the beef is not thinly sliced but cut into fairly large pieces, each about 150 g in weight. Each piece is lightly scored, then boiled over low heat until almost tender.

Kari Kepala Ikan Jenahak

Preparation: 20 minutes Cooking: 30 minutes

Ingredients

Mangrove red snapper (*ikan jenahak*) head	1 kg
Salt	as needed
Cooking oil	3 Tbsp
Shallots	4, peeled and sliced
Garlic	3 cloves, peeled and sliced
Black peas	1/2 tsp
Curry leaves	3 sprigs, stems discarded
Coconut cream	250 ml, squeezed from 1 grated coconut with a little water added
Coconut milk	500 ml, squeezed from same grated coconut with sufficient water added
Tamarind pulp (*asam Jawa*)	1 Tbsp, mixed with 125 ml water and strained
Aubergines (eggplants/ brinjals)	2, diagonally cut into thick slices

Spices

Fennel seeds (*jintan manis biji*)	1/2 tsp
Mustard seeds	1/2 tsp
Fenugreek seeds (*halba*)	1 tsp

Ingredients to be ground

Dried chillies	30, soaked
Coriander seeds (*ketumbar biji*)	1 Tbsp
Cumin seeds (*jintan putih biji*)	1 dsp
Black peppercorns	2 tsp
Turmeric (*kunyit*)	1.25-cm knob, peeled
Shallots	10, peeled
Garlic	4 cloves, peeled

Method

- Rub fish head with 1 tsp salt and leave for 15 minutes.
- Heat oil in a wok. Fry shallot and garlic slices, black peas, curry leaves and spices until fragrant.
- Add ground ingredients and fry until fragrant and oil separates.
- Pour in coconut milk and tamarind juice and bring to a slow boil.
- Add aubergines and simmer for 5 minutes, then add fish head and cook over low heat for 12–15 minutes.
- Add coconut cream and salt. Bring to a slow boil, stirring gently.

Gulai Daging

Preparation: 20 minutes Cooking: 45 minutes

Ingredients

Beef	600 g
Cooking oil	3 Tbsp
Onion	1, peeled and sliced
Garlic	3 cloves, peeled and sliced
Cinnamon (*kayu manis*)	1.25-cm stick
Star anise (*bunga lawang*)	2 sections
Coconut cream	250 ml, squeezed from 1 grated coconut with a little water added
Coconut milk	625 ml, squeezed from same grated coconut with sufficient water added
Potatoes	3, peeled and cut into wedges
Salt	1 tsp

Ingredients to be ground

Dried chillies	30, soaked
Shallots	12, peeled
Garlic	3 cloves, peeled
Ginger	2.5-cm knob, peeled
Turmeric (*kunyit*)	2.5-cm knob, peeled
Fennel seeds (*jintan manis biji*)	1 rounded (heaped) tsp
Cumin seeds (*jintan putih biji*)	1 tsp
Black peppercorns	1 tsp
Cinnamon (*kayu manis*)	1.25-cm stick
Star anise (*bunga lawang*)	3 sections
Cardamoms (*buah pelaga*)	3

Method

- Cut beef into thin slices. Set aside.
- Heat oil in a wok. Fry onion, garlic, cinnamon and star anise until fragrant.
- Add ground ingredients and fry over low heat until fragrant and oil separates.
- Add beef slices and stir-fry for 5 minutes, then pour in coconut milk. Simmer for 15 minutes.
- Add potatoes and cook until meat is tender and potatoes soft.
- Add coconut cream and salt. Bring to a slow boil, stirring gently

Rendang Ayam

Preparation: 20 minutes Cooking: 30 minutes

Ingredients

Chicken	1, about 1.5 kg, cut into small pieces
Tamarind pulp (*asam Jawa*)	1 Tbsp, mixed with 250 ml water and strained
Light soy sauce	2 Tbsp
Salt	1 tsp
Cooking oil	5 Tbsp
Lemon grass (*serai*)	2 stalks, lightly crushed

Ingredients to be ground

Dried chillies	30, soaked
Shallots	15, peeled
Garlic	4 cloves, peeled
Ginger	2.5-cm knob, peeled
Turmeric (*kunyit*)	2.5-cm knob, peeled
Black peppercorns	1 tsp

Method

- Into a mixing bowl, put chicken, ground ingredients, tamarind juice, light soy sauce and salt. Mix well and leave for 30 minutes.
- Heat oil in a wok and fry lemon grass until fragrant.
- Put in chicken and fry over moderate heat for 5 minutes.
- Reduce heat, cover and simmer, stirring occasionally, until chicken is tender and gravy quite dry.

Gulai Ayam

Preparation: 20 minutes Cooking: 40 minutes

Ingredients

Chicken	1, 1.5 kg, cut into bite-size pieces
Salt	as needed
Cooking oil	3 Tbsp
Coconut cream	250 ml, squeezed from 1 grated coconut with a little water added
Coconut milk	750 ml, squeezed from same grated coconut with sufficient water added

Ingredients to be sliced

Shallots	4, peeled
Garlic	2 cloves, peeled
Ginger	2.5-cm knob, peeled

Spices

Star anise (*bunga lawang*)	2 sections
Cloves (*bunga cengkih*)	2
Cinnamon (*kayu manis*)	1.25-cm stick

Ingredients to be ground

Dried chillies	30, soaked
Coriander seeds (*ketumbar biji*)	1 Tbsp
Fennel seeds (*jintan manis biji*)	1 tsp
Cumin seeds (*jintan putih biji*)	1/2 tsp
Shallots	10, peeled
Garlic	2 cloves, peeled
Turmeric (*kunyit*)	2.5-cm knob, peeled

Method

- Season chicken with 1 tsp salt and leave for 15 minutes.
- Heat oil in a wok. Fry sliced ingredients and spices until fragrant.
- Add ground ingredients and fry until fragrant and oil separates.
- Add chicken and stir-fry for 3 minutes, then add coconut milk. Simmer over low heat until meat is tender.
- Add coconut cream and 1 tsp salt. Simmer for 5 minutes more.

Kerabu Tauge with Tripe or Cockles

Preparation: 30 minutes Cooking: 1 hour

Ingredients

Tripe	600 g, or 1 kg cockles
Slaked lime	1 tsp, for tripe only
Ginger	2.5-cm knob, lightly crushed, for tripe only
Bean sprouts (*tauge*)	600 g, tailed
Rice	60 g, roasted until lightly browned and ground
Onions	2, peeled and finely sliced
Tamarind pulp (*asam Jawa*)	1 tsp, mixed with 2 Tbsp water and strained
Salt	1 1/2 tsp
Skinned coconut	1/2, grated, for *kerisik* (page 11)
Pure coconut cream (*pati santan*)	squeezed from 1/2 grated coconut

Ingredients to be ground

Red chillies	6, coarsely ground
Ginger	2.5-cm knob, peeled
Lemon grass (*serai*)	3 stalks
Galangal (*lengkuas*)	2 slices, peeled
Dried prawn (shrimp) paste (*belacan*)	2.5-cm square piece, toasted
Black peppercorns	1 tsp

Method

- Wash tripe and rub with slaked lime, then rinse well.
- Into a saucepan, put tripe and ginger and add enough water to cover. Then, boil over low heat for 1 hour or until trip is tender. Alternatively, pressure cook for 30 minutes.
- Drain cooked tripe and thinly slice when cool.
- If using cockles, scald in boiling hot water and extract flesh from shells. Set aside.
- Scald bean sprouts in boiling water for 1 minute. Drain well and combine with tripe or cockles in a large bowl.
- Mix in ground ingredients, ground rice, onions, tamarind juice, salt and *kerisik*. Just before serving, add coconut cream.

Tepung Bungkus

Preparation: 30 minutes   Cooking: 30 minutes

Ingredients

Rice flour	240 g
Water	500 ml
Coconut milk	750 ml, squeezed from 1 grated coconut with sufficient water added
Sugar	210 g
Salt	1/4 tsp
Screwpine (*pandan*) leaves	2, washed and knotted
Banana leaves	16, cut into 18 x 15-cm pieces and scalded
Filling*	1 recipe

Method

- Sift rice flour into a bowl, add water and blend until smooth.
- In a saucepan, combine coconut milk, sugar, salt and screwpine leaves. Cook over low heat and stir to dissolve sugar.
- Add rice flour batter and, using a wooden spoon, stir for about 5 minutes or until mixture is cooked and a smooth paste. Remove from heat.
- Onto the centre of each banana leaf, put 1 dessertspoonful cooked dough mixture.
- Fold over one side of leaf to flatten dough into a small rectangle. Top with 2 balls of filling at the centre, about 1.25 cm apart.
- Cover filling with another dessertspoonful of dough mixture.
- Fold banana leaf in thirds lengthways, to overlap over mixture. Fold and tuck short ends under. Repeat until ingredients are used up.
- Steam parcels for 20 minutes. Serve hot or cold.

*Filling

Palm sugar (*gula Melaka*)	90 g, chopped
Water	125 ml
Grated young coconut	180 g
Salt	1/4 tsp

Method

- Into a small saucepan, put palm sugar and water. Cook over low heat, stirring until sugar dissolves. Strain.
- In a wok, combine strained syrup, grated coconut and salt. Fry until coconut is evenly coated with syrup. Dish out.
- Shape cooled filling into marble-size balls.

Kobis or Tauge Masak Putih

Preparation: 10 minutes Cooking 15 minutes

Ingredients

Cabbage (*kobis*)	300 g, or 300 g tailed bean sprouts
Coconut cream	125 ml, squeezed from 1/2 grated coconut with a little water added
Coconut milk	1 litre, squeezed from same grated coconut with sufficient water added
Prawns (shrimps)	300 g, small and peeled
Salt	1/2 tsp
Spring onion (scallion)	1, chopped

Ingredients to be sliced

Red chillies	5
Shallots	6, peeled
Garlic	1 clove, peeled

Method

- Cut cabbage into 1.25-cm pieces.
- In a wok, combine coconut milk and sliced ingredients.
- Bring to a slow boil. Simmer for 5 minutes more, then add cabbage.
- When cabbage is soft, add prawns and coconut cream and salt. Add spring onion last.
- If using bean sprouts, put in prawns first, then add bean sprouts and coconut cream. Remove from heat as soon as liquid reaches the boil.

Sabah & Sarawak

Sabah and Sarawak form the states of East Malaysia. Compared to other Malaysian states, Sabah is sparsely populated but is extremely rich in natural resources like timber and oil. Popularly known as the "land of below the wind", the world's oldest jungles offering a colourful profusion of exotic tropical flora and fauna are found there. Kadazans form the largest indigenous group; among others like Muruts, Rungus, etc.

Sarawak, the "land of the hornbill", has its capital, Kuching, perched on the banks of the Sarawak River. On the southern shore lie the business district and port facilities, characterised by Chinese shophouses. The northern shore is predominantly populated by Malays. Their lifestyle evolves along water villages of wooden houses rather precariously perched on stilts above the tidal Sarawak River. Ibans form the largest indigenous group here, and these hardworking people live in communal longhouses throughout the jungles.

The range of cuisine offered to the adventurous person is mainly Malay and Chinese, with superb fresh seafood. Malay cuisine is simple but remarkably tasty. Dried prawn paste is a popular ingredient and moderately used for sweetness and flavour. Cakes are extremely popular, particularly steamed cakes, which are very rich and the main attraction during festive occasions.

Sambal Santan Udang

Preparation: 20 minutes   Cooking: 10 minutes

Ingredients

Prawns (shrimps)	600 g, medium
Cooking oil	3 Tbsp
Coconut milk	315 ml, squeezed from 1/2 grated coconut with sufficient water added
Tamarind pulp (*asam Jawa*)	1 rounded (heaped) dsp, mixed with 65 ml water and strained
Salt	1 rounded (heaped) tsp or to taste

Ingredients to be ground

Red chillies	10
Onions	2, peeled
Garlic	4 cloves, peeled
Lemon grass (*serai*)	4 stalks
Ginger	2.5-cm knob, peeled
Turmeric (*kunyit*)	2.5-cm knob, peeled
Dried prawn (shrimp) paste (*belacan*)	1.25-cm square piece

Method

- Wash and clean prawns, then peel but leave tails intact.
- Heat oil and fry ground ingredients until fragrant and oil separates.
- Add coconut milk and bring to a slow boil.
- Put in peeled prawns, tamarind juice and salt to taste. Simmer for 5 minutes or until prawns are cooked.

Umai (Raw Fish Sambal)

Preparation: 15 minutes

Ingredients

Threadfin (*ikan kurau*)	300 g, small
Roselle (*asam paya*)	8, ripe, hard outer skins and seeds removed, or *asam kelubi*
Bird's eye chillies (*cili padi*)	30, ground
Shallots	8, peeled and sliced
Garlic	4 cloves, peeled and sliced
Ginger	2.5-cm knob, peeled and chopped
Salt	1 tsp

Method

- Wash and debone fish. Cut into slices and set aside.
- Chop roselle and combine with chillies, shallots, garlic and ginger.
- Mix fish slices with combined ingredients and salt. Leave for 10 minutes.
- Serve with rice and 1–2 other dishes.

Udang Masak Merah

Preparation: 10 minutes Cooking: 10 minutes

Ingredients

Freshwater prawns (shrimps) (*udang galah*)	1 kg, or king prawns
Salt	as needed
Ground white pepper	1/2 tsp
Cooking oil	100 ml
Tomatoes	4, quartered
Sugar	1 tsp

Ingredients to be ground

Dried chillies	30–35, soaked
Shallots	12, peeled
Garlic	8 cloves, peeled
Galangal (*lengkuas*)	4-cm knob, peeled
Dried prawn (shrimp) paste (*belacan*)	2.5-cm square piece

Method

- Clean prawns and trim off sharp ends of feelers and legs. Leave unpeeled.
- Season prawns with 2 tsp salt and pepper. Leave for 30 minutes.
- Heat oil in a wok. Fry ground ingredients over low heat until fragrant.
- Add prawns, increasing heat at the same time. Stir-fry prawns, then add tomatoes. Sprinkle in a little water if too dry.
- Add 1 tsp salt and sugar. When prawns turn bright red, they are cooked.

Rendang Daging

Preparation: 15 minutes   Cooking: 2 hours

Ingredients

Beef	600 g, cut into 4-cm long thin slices
Coconut milk	1 litre, squeezed from 1 grated coconut with sufficient water added
Salt	$1^{1}/_{2}$ tsp or to taste

Ingredients to be ground

Dried chillies	20, soaked
Shallots	10, peeled
Lemon grass (*serai*)	3 stalks
Galangal (*lengkuas*)	2.5-cm knob, peeled
Ginger	2.5-cm knob, peeled
Turmeric (*kunyit*)	2.5-cm knob, peeled

Method

- Into a pot, put beef, ground ingredients and coconut milk.
- Simmer, uncovered, for 2 hours or until meat is tender and gravy thick.
- Add salt to taste.

Ayam Masak Asam Pedas

Preparation: 20 minutes   Cooking: 30 minutes

Ingredients

Chicken	1, about 1.5 kg, cut into bite-size pieces
Salt	as needed
Cooking oil	125 ml
Coconut milk	750 ml, squeezed from 1 grated coconut with sufficient water added
Canned pineapple cubes	2 cans (each 567 g)

Ingredients to be ground

Dried chillies	25, soaked
Shallots	10
Garlic	6 cloves, peeled
Candlenuts (*buah keras*)	3
Ginger	2.5-cm knob, peeled
Galangal (*lengkuas*)	2.5-cm knob, peeled
Lemon grass (*serai*)	1 stalk
Ground coriander (*ketumbar serbuk*)	2 Tbsp
Ground turmeric (*kunyit serbuk*)	1 tsp

Method

- Season chicken with 1 tsp salt and leave for 30 minutes.
- Heat oil and fry ground ingredients until fragrant and oil separates.
- Add chicken and fry for 2 minutes, then pour in coconut milk and bring to a slow boil.
- Add pineapple cubes and simmer for 20 minutes or until chicken is tender. Add salt to taste.

Ayam Masak Putih

Preparation: 15 minutes   Cooking: 20 minutes

Ingredients

Chicken	1/2, about 1 kg, cut into bite-size pieces
Salt	as needed
Cooking oil	3 Tbsp
Coconut cream	250 ml, squeezed from 1/2 grated coconut with a little water added
Coconut milk	500 ml, squeezed from same grated coconut with sufficient water added
Tomatoes	2, quartered

Ingredients to be ground

Shallots	6, peeled
Garlic	4 cloves, peeled
Ginger	2.5-cm knob, peeled
Galangal (*lengkuas*)	2.5-cm knob, peeled
White peppercorns	1/2 Tbsp
Black peppercorns	1/2 Tbsp

Method

- Season chicken with 1 tsp salt and leave for 30 minutes.
- Heat oil in a wok. Fry ground ingredients until fragrant and oil separates.
- Add chicken and fry for 2–3 minutes, then add coconut milk and bring to the boil.
- Add tomatoes and simmer for 15 minutes or until chicken is tender.
- Add coconut cream and salt to taste.

Ayam Masak Kicap

Preparation: 15 minutes Cooking: 25 minutes

Ingredients

Chicken	1/2, about 1 kg, cut into bite-size pieces
Salt	as needed
Allspice	1/2 dsp
Dark soy sauce	1/2 Tbsp
Cooking oil	3 Tbsp
Water	190 ml
Onions	2, peeled and sliced
Red chillies	2, sliced

Ingredients to be ground

Shallots	6, peeled
Garlic	4 cloves, peeled
Ginger	2.5-cm knob, peeled
Black peppercorns	1/2 Tbsp
White peppercorns	1/2 Tbsp

Method

- Season chicken with 1 tsp salt, allspice and dark soy sauce. Leave for 1 hour.
- Heat oil and fry ground ingredients until fragrant.
- Add chicken and fry for 3 minutes, then add water and bring to the boil. Cover and simmer gently for 15 minutes or until chicken is tender.
- Add onions and chillies and stir-fry until gravy is thick. Add salt to taste.

Tauge Tumis

Preparation: 10 minutes Cooking: 5 minutes

Ingredients

Cooking oil	3 Tbsp
Shallots	2, peeled and sliced
Garlic	1 clove, peeled and sliced
Firm bean curd (*tau kwa*)	2, cut into 1.25-cm cubes
Bean sprouts (*tauge*)	300 g, tailed
Chinese (garlic) chives	12 stalks, cut into 4-cm lengths
Salt	1/2 tsp
Red chilli	1, sliced

Ingredients to be ground

Dried anchovies (*ikan bilis*)	30 g, heads and entrails discarded if desired
Dried prawn (shrimp) paste (*belacan*)	1.25-cm square piece

Method

- Heat oil in a wok, then lightly brown shallots and garlic.
- Add ground ingredients and fry over low heat until fragrant.
- Add bean curd, increasing heat at the same time and stir-fry. Sprinkle in a little water if too dry.
- Add bean sprouts and stir-fry for 1 minute, then add Chinese chives, salt and red chilli. Stir-fry quickly to mix ingredients. Serve hot.

Kek Masam Manis

Preparation: 20 minutes Steaming: 42 minutes

Ingredients

Eggs	5, separated
Castor (superfine) sugar	150 g
Butter	250 g
Condensed milk	$^1/_2$ can (397 g)
Vanilla essence (extract)	1 tsp
Soda crackers	150 g, milled or pounded and sifted
Green food colouring	$^1/_4$ tsp
Haw flakes	15 packets

Method

- Whisk egg whites until stiff. Gradually add in sugar, a spoonful at a time, beating well after each addition.
- In a separate bowl, cream butter, condensed milk and vanilla essence until light and fluffy. Add egg yolks, one at a time, beating well after each addition.
- Add egg yolk mixture to egg white mixture. Combine lightly and evenly, then fold in milled crackers. Divide mixture into 2 equal portions and colour one green.
- Line base of a 21-cm round cake tin with greased greaseproof paper. Then, evenly spread on one-third of green mixture atop paper lining. Arrange 3 packets of haw flakes on the surface. Steam over rapidly boiling water for 7 minutes.
- Remove cake tin from steamer and spread on one-third of uncoloured mixture over steamed layer. Arrange 3 packets of haw flakes on top and steam for 7 minutes.
- When done, repeat process with green mixture, then uncoloured mixture. Resulting cake should have alternating layers of colour and haw flakes.
- Leave completed cake to cool in the tin for 15 minutes before turning out onto a wire rack. Allow to cool thoroughly before cutting.

Note: Haw flakes are thin red flakes the size of a 20-cent coin. Made in China and sold in most local sweet shops, they are sweet-and-sour and a favourite of most children.

Bubur Pedas

Preparation: 30 minutes   Cooking: 30 minutes

Ingredients

Rice	120 g, washed and drained
Grated coconut	90 g
Water	500 ml
Cooking oil	3 Tbsp
Shallots	2, peeled and sliced
Garlic	1 clove, peeled and sliced
Coconut cream	250 ml, squeezed from 1/2 grated coconut with a little water added
Coconut milk	750 ml, squeezed from same grated coconut with sufficient water added
Small peeled prawns (shrimps) or beef	300 g, cut into small pieces
Dried Chinese mushrooms	4, soaked to soften, stems discarded and diced
Bean curd sticks (*fu chok*)	45 g, soaked and cut into small pieces
Salt	2 rounded (heaped) tsp or to taste

Ingredients to be chopped

Shallots	3, peeled
Garlic	2 cloves, peeled
Dried chillies	5, soaked and seeded
Lemon grass (*serai*)	1 stalk
Ginger	2.5-cm knob, peeled
Galangal (*lengkuas*)	2.5-cm knob, peeled
Turmeric (*kunyit*)	2.5-cm knob, peeled

Ingredients to be finely ground

Coriander seeds (*ketumbar biji*)	1 Tbsp, roasted
Cumin seeds (*jintan putih biji*)	1 tsp, roasted
Fennel seeds (*jintan manis biji*)	1 tsp, roasted
Cinnamon (*kayu manis*)	1.25-cm stick
Star anise (*bunga lawang*)	4 sections
Cardamom (*buah pelaga*)	1

Method

- Into a wok, put rice, grated coconut and chopped ingredients. Roast over low heat for 10 minutes or until fragrant and lightly browned.
- Transfer rice mixture to a blender (food processor) and blend with 500 ml water. Leave to soak for 20 minutes. Alternatively, pound roasted ingredients until fine before soaking in 500 ml water.
- Heat oil in a pot and lightly brown shallots and garlic. Add rice mixture, ground spices and coconut milk. Bring to a slow boil, stirring frequently.
- Add prawns or beef, mushrooms, bean curd sticks and return to the boil. Simmer for 5 minutes more, then add coconut cream and salt to taste.

Note: *Bubur pedas* is popular with the Muslims in Sarawak especially during the fasting month. Prepared *bubur pedas* ingredients are readily available in small packets.

Kek Kukus Sri Kaya

Preparation: 15 minutes Steaming: 50 minutes

Ingredients

Plain (all-purpose) flour	180 g
Baking powder	1 tsp
Butter	180 g
Castor (superfine) sugar	150 g
Evaporated milk	4 Tbsp
Egg jam (*kaya*)	4 Tbsp
Golden syrup	1 Tbsp
Vanilla essence (extract)	1 tsp
Egg yolks	5, large
Green food colouring	a few drops

Method

- Sift flour and baking powder into a bowl. Set aside.
- Cream butter and sugar until light and fluffy, then beat in evaporated milk, egg jam, golden syrup and vanilla essence.
- Add egg yolks, one at a time, and beat well. Then, fold in sifted flour and mix well.
- Divide mixture into 2 equal portions and stir green colouring into one.
- Grease a 20-cm round cake tin with butter. Put in half the green batter and spread out evenly, smoothening with the back of a spoon.
- Top green layer with half the uncoloured batter and spread out evenly again. Repeat with remaining green batter, then uncoloured for alternating colours.
- Prepare a steamer for use. When water is rapidly boiling, put in filled cake tin and steam for 50 minutes.
- When done, carefully turn out onto a wire rack to cool before cutting.

Kek Cream Soda

Preparation: 15 minutes Baking: 35 minutes

Ingredients

Butter	180 g
Eggs	3, large
Castor (superfine) sugar	90 g
Vanilla or lemon essence (extract)	1 tsp
Ice cream soda	250 ml

Ingredients to be sifted together

Plain (all-purpose) flour	240 g
Baking powder	1 tsp

Method

- Beat butter until light and creamy.
- In a separate bowl, whisk eggs and castor sugar until light and fluffy. Stir in beaten butter and essence.
- Carefully fold in sifted ingredients alternately with ice cream soda.
- Pour mixture into a 21-cm round cake tin lined with greased greaseproof paper.
- Bake in an oven preheated to 175°C/350°F for 35 minutes or until cooked when tested with a skewer.

Kek Embun Pagi

Preparation: 20 minutes Steaming: 45 minutes

Ingredients

Plain (all-purpose) flour	240 g+ 150 g, sifted
Baking powder	1 tsp
Butter	250 g
Castor (superfine) sugar	270 g
Eggs	8, separated
Condensed milk	3/4 can (397 g)
Almond essence (extract)	1/4 tsp
Green food colouring	a few drops
Red food colouring	a few drops
Yellow food colouring (optional)	a few drops
Almond flakes	60 g
Vanilla essence (extract)	1 tsp
Red cherries	10, sliced

Method

- Sift 240 g flour and baking powder into a bowl. Set aside.
- Cream butter and 150 g sugar until light and fluffy. Add egg yolks, one at a time, beating well after each addition.
- Add condensed milk and almond essence and cream further until light and creamy. Fold in sifted flour and baking powder, half at a time.
- Divide mixture into 3 equal parts. Into one, blend a few drops of green colouring. Into another, blend a few drops of red colouring. Either leave the third plain or blend in a few drops of yellow colouring.
- Line a 25-cm, round cake tin with greased greaseproof paper. Spoon in green mixture and spread evenly. Steam over rapid boiling water for 10 minutes or until cake is firm to the touch.
- Remove cake tin from steamer and sprinkle on half the almond flakes. Spread yellow mixture on top and steam for 10 minutes again.
- On top of cooked yellow layer, sprinkle remaining almond flakes and top with red mixture, also to be steamed for 10 minutes.
- Whisk egg whites until just stiff. Gradually beat in 120 g sugar, half at a time, beating well after each addition. Add vanilla essence. Carefully fold in 150 g sifted flour and mix well.
- Spoon egg white mixture over steamed cake and spread evenly and smoothly. Arrange cherry slices on top and steam again for 12 minutes.
- Allow cake to cool in tin for 15 minutes before turning out onto a wire rack to cool completely.

Madu Kemeyan

Preparation: 20 minutes Steaming: 40 minutes

Ingredients

Butter	250 g
Castor (superfine) sugar	as needed
Brown sugar	1 Tbsp
Eggs	5, separated
Horlicks	120 g
Soda crackers	60 g, milled or pounded and sifted
Cocoa	2 Tbsp, sifted
Golden syrup	1 Tbsp
Condensed milk	3 Tbsp
Plain (all-purpose) flour	90 g, sifted

Method

- Cream 125 g butter with 60 g castor sugar and brown sugar until light and fluffy. Add egg yolks, one at a time, beating well after each addition. Then, stir in Horlicks, soda crackers, cocoa and golden syrup.
- In a second bowl, cream 125 g butter with condensed milk until light and fluffy. Set aside.
- In a third bowl, whisk egg whites until stiff. Then, gradually beat in 120 g castor sugar, a spoonful at a time, beating well after each addition. Stir in condensed milk mixture. Carefully fold in sifted flour and mix well.
- Line base of a 21-cm round cake tin with greased greaseproof paper. Spread 7–8 dessertspoonfuls of egg white mixture evenly over lining. Steam over rapidly boiling water for 8 minutes or until cake is firm to the touch.
- Remove cake tin from steamer. Drop alternate spoonfuls of egg white and chocolate mixture, 1.25 cm apart, over steamed surface. Return cake tin to steamer and steam for 10 minutes.
- Repeat dropping-and-steaming process with both mixtures until they are used up. Allow cake to cool in cake tin for 15 minutes before turning out onto a wire rack to cool completely.

Weights & Measures

Metric and American (spoon and cup) measures are used throughout this book. All measures are level except when stated otherwise. However, measures for liquid do not have to be adhered to precisely as different cookers vary in heat intensity. A little extra liquid can be added, for instance, if meat is not properly cooked. Quantities for salt or sugar can be changed according to individual taste.

LIQUID AND VOLUME MEASURES

Metric	Imperial	American
5 ml	1/6 fl oz	1 teaspoon
10 ml	1/3 fl oz	1 dessertspoon
15 ml	1/2 fl oz	1 tablespoon
60 ml	2 fl oz	1/4 cup (4 tablespoons)
85 ml	2 1/2 fl oz	1/3 cup
90 ml	3 fl oz	3/8 cup (6 tablespoons)
125 ml	4 fl oz	1/2 cup
180 ml	6 fl oz	3/4 cup
250 ml	8 fl oz	1 cup
300 ml	10 fl oz (1/2 pint)	1 1/4 cups
375 ml	12 fl oz	1 1/2 cups
435 ml	14 fl oz	1 3/4 cups
500 ml	16 fl oz	2 cups
625 ml	20 fl oz (1 pint)	2 1/2 cups
750 ml	24 fl oz (1 1/5 pints)	3 cups
1 litre	32 fl oz (1 3/5 pints)	4 cups
1.25 litres	40 fl oz (2 pints)	5 cups
1.5 litres	48 fl oz (2 2/5 pints)	6 cups
2.5 litres	80 fl oz (4 pints)	10 cups

DRY MEASURES

Metric	Imperial
30 grams	1 ounce
45 grams	1 1/2 ounces
55 grams	2 ounces
70 grams	2 1/2 ounces
85 grams	3 ounces
100 grams	3 1/2 ounces
110 grams	4 ounces
125 grams	4 1/2 ounces
140 grams	5 ounces
280 grams	10 ounces
450 grams	16 ounces (1 pound)
500 grams	1 pound, 1 1/2 ounces
700 grams	1 1/2 pounds
800 grams	1 3/4 pounds
1 kilogram	2 pounds, 3 ounces
1.5 kilograms	3 pounds, 4 1/2 ounces
2 kilograms	4 pounds, 6 ounces

OVEN TEMPERATURE

	°C	°F	Gas Regulo
Very slow	120	250	1
Slow	150	300	2
Moderately slow	160	325	3
Moderate	180	350	4
Moderately hot	190/200	370/400	5/6
Hot	210/220	410/440	6/7
Very hot	230	450	8
Super hot	250/290	475/550	9/10

LENGTH

Metric	Imperial
0.5 cm	1/4 inch
1 cm	1/2 inch
1.5 cm	3/4 inch
2.5 cm	1 inch